RECONSTRUCTING EUROPE, 45 YEARS AFTER YALTA

The Charter of Paris (1990)

Preface by Jean-Yves LE DRIAN
Minister for Europe and Foreign Affairs

Edited by Nicolas BADALASSI and Jean-Philippe DUMAS
With the participation of Frédéric BOZO and Pierre GROSSER
And with the contribution of Pauline CHERBONNIER

Archives Directorate
Ministry for Europe and Foreign Affairs

CTHS
The Comité des Travaux Historiques et Scientifiques
is an institute affiliated with the École Nationale des Chartes

Photograph on the cover: Plenary Assembly of the CSCE in the Conference Room of the Ministry for Europe and Foreign Affairs, Avenue Kléber, 19 November 1990. Archives of the Ministry for Europe and Foreign Affairs, La Courneuve, image collection. © Frédéric de la Mure/Ministry for Europe and Foreign Affairs

All rights reserved for all countries. Any full or partial reproduction, by whatever means, of documents published in this book is prohibited, except with the authorization of the Ministry for Europe and Foreign Affairs and the Comité des Travaux Historiques et Scientifiques. Only reproduction that is reserved for the use of the copyist and not intended for collective use is authorized, and small quotes justified by the scientific and informative nature of the work in which it is incorporated (art. L. 122-4, L. 122-5 and L. 335-2 of the French Code of Intellectual Property).

© Archives Directorate of the Ministry for Europe and Foreign Affairs, Paris, 2020 and the Comité des Travaux Historiques et Scientifiques

Translators: Lucy Arbuckle, Diane Bertrand, Meegan Davis, in-house translators and revisers from the Translation Unit of the Ministry for Europe and Foreign Affairs

Printer: Chirat

ISBN 978-2-7355-0923-2

Printed at Saint-Just-la-Pendue
Registration of copyright: Bibliothèque Nationale de France (4th quarter 2020)

PREFACE

Thirty years after its publication, it is essential that we now reread the *Charter of Paris for a New Europe*.

Not only because it poignantly sets out the "*historic expectations*" of a "*time of profound change*" in which the face of our continent was transformed in just a few months, beginning the march towards reunification after several decades of tragic division. But also because it poses a crucial question to us French and Europeans today: what have we done with the "*new beginning*" called for by thirty-four Heads of State and Government in Paris in November 1990?

*

The historians and distinguished observers who contributed to this work have tackled this question head on. Because there is no doubt that not all of the Charter's promises have been kept.

It clearly had a symbolic value and even before its adoption served as a catalyst for major negotiations of the time, on German reunification and the Treaty on Conventional Armed Forces in Europe. By paving the way for the institutionalization of the Conference on Security and Co-operation in Europe (CSCE)[1], which would five years later become the OSCE, it was an important milestone in the construction of multilateralism. This undeniable progress confirmed the importance of a text which undoubtedly remains a reference.

However, slowly but surely, the ambition to implement the security architecture called for by the Charter of Paris petered out. Instability began to resurface as regulatory instruments were dismantled one by one – from confidence-building measures to arms control and reduction treaties. Gradually, a dangerous vacuum opened up. And now, the risk of conflict once more hangs over our continent. This has been plain to see from Russia's destabilizing actions over the last decade. In Georgia, and then Ukraine, we have seen military confrontation return to Europe.

---

[1] Conference on Security and Co-operation in Europe (CSCE): a forum for negotiation between the two Cold War blocs, active from 1973 until 1994.

We have witnessed the use of chemical weapons in a European city. Cyber attacks have been perpetrated to undermine democratic life in our countries. In a sense, these major retrograde steps confirm the truth in the conviction set out throughout the Charter that, *"in order to strengthen peace and security among our States, the advancement of democracy, and respect for and effective exercise of human rights, are indispensable"*. We cannot make the link any clearer between democratic principles and humanistic values on the one hand and building our collective European security on the other. And when political opponents are threatened, when the integrity of electoral processes is flouted, it clearly becomes extremely difficult to hold the confidence-building dialogue that we still need throughout the continent in order to realistically seek the ways and means to finally implement the Ten Principles of the Helsinki Final Act, which were recalled in 1990 in the Charter of Paris.

*

It is now up to Europeans to improve on what was attempted thirty years ago. It is a task for both the present and the future, which we will not be able to undertake without a solid sense of the lessons and complexities of the past.

So that, in my view, is the immense value of the contributions compiled in this work by the French Foreign Ministry's Archives Directorate. Let us hope they help us quickly rediscover the meaning and sense of urgency of the Charter.

Jean-Yves Le Drian
Minister for Europe and Foreign Affairs

Pierre GROSSER[*]
THE CHARTER OF PARIS AND THE HISTORY OF THE END OF THE COLD WAR

The Charter of Paris rarely gets a mention in the history of the end of the Cold War. Yet it sheds light on the timeline of events running from 1988 to 1991, which are often reduced to a chronological milestone marking the end of what is seen as a bygone, homogeneous historical chain of events: the Cold War. It also elucidates the shifts in the interpretations of this major "turning point" in modern history.

- ***Resituating the Charter of Paris in the chronology of events at the end of the Cold War***

The history of the Cold War started with neither a declaration of war nor military combat and ended with neither an armistice, military surrender nor a grand peace treaty signed by all protagonists. It can be marked out with different start and end dates depending on the interpretation made as to what it really was. The maximum timeframe traditionally given ties in with the history of the Bolshevik revolution and the Soviet Union, spanning from October 1917 to December 1991. However, talk in recent years of a "new cold war" between the "West" and Russia or China has lengthened the timeline. If China (not to mention North Korea and Cuba) remains fundamentally communist, then the ideological rivalry extends beyond the end of the communist regimes in Europe. For those who believe that the communist regimes perverted the communist ideal and were not communist, the history of struggle against capitalism, and allegedly kindred imperialism, started well before 1917 and continues to this day. If the history of Eurasia from the 18th and especially the 19th centuries onwards is marked by the intent to contain Russian ambitions, real or imagined, and the United States really did simply take over from the British Empire, then the Cold War is merely one episode in these geopolitics of powers.

---

[*] Sciences Po Paris.

So which dates are commonly accepted as the bounds downstream of the history of the Cold War? Two of them concern the CSCE. Historian Sarah Snyder points to January 1989, when the Vienna meeting showed real progress in a development seen as evidence of the Soviet Union's "socialisation".[1] When the follow-up meeting opened in November 1986, Soviet Foreign Affairs Minister Eduard Shevardnadze had astounded the gathering by proposing that a meeting on "humanitarian issues" be held in Moscow. One French senior official saw this as "tantamount to celebrating a first communion in a brothel."[2] French diplomats strived to forestall the proposal while gratifying Moscow with the holding of a conference,[3] which took place in September 1991 in a city still marked by the attempted coup of 19-21 August.

The second date concerns the Charter of Paris for a New Europe, signed in Paris by thirty-four countries in November 1990, which could be equated with an old-style peace congress, attended by all the players to bring an end to a conflict, but also with the conferences at the end of the two world wars, since it set out to codify common principles and values and outline institutional developments for the European order. Nevertheless, as François Mitterrand put it, the difference was that there were neither victors nor vanquished, but "free countries equal in dignity" and, for the first time, the changes on the European continent were not the outcome of a war or a bloody revolution. As Jean Musitelli wrote, the Charter "solemnly buries the Cold War." And indeed it stipulates that, "The era of confrontation and division of Europe has ended." As one American diplomat who later took part in OSCE missions saw it, the Charter, taken together with the documents produced by the June 1990 Copenhagen Meeting of the Conference on the Human Dimension of the CSCE, constituted a "normative achievement and commitment unmatched since the adoption by the United Nations General Assembly of the Universal Declaration of Human Rights."[4]

Yet these two dates, January 1989 and November 1991, are rarely mentioned. 1989 remains the symbol of the "acceleration" and unpredictability of history while the opening and subsequent destruction of the Berlin Wall are strong images of European upheaval.[5] The West won the battle of history with these pictures of peoples

---

[1] Sarah Snyder, *Human Rights Activism and the End of the Cold War*, Cambridge, Cambridge University Press, 2011 Also, Andrea Brait and Michael Gehler, "The CSCE Vienna Follow-up Meeting and Alois Mock, 1986-1989", In: Michael Gehler et al. (eds.). *Christian Democracy and the Fall of Communism*, Leiden University Press, 2020, Chapter 2, and Nicolas Badalassi and Sarah Snyder (eds.), *The CSCE and the End of the Cold War*, New York, Berghahn, 2018.

[2] Jacques Andreani, *Helsinki: le piège*, Paris, Odile Jacob, 2005, p. 170.

[3] Memorandum for the President, 7 July 1987, Archives Nationales, 5AG4 DG87, cited in Pierre Grosser, "François Mitterrand et le bloc de l'Est, 1984-1998", In: Georges Saunier (Ed.) *Mitterrand. Les années d'alternance*, Paris, Nouveau Monde, 2019.

[4] William H. Hill, *No Place for Russia. European Security Institutions since 1989*, New York, Columbia University Press, 2018, Chapter 2.

[5] Pierre Grosser, *1989. L'année où le monde a basculé*, Paris, Perrin/Tempus, 2e ed., 2019.

who, irresistibly drawn to it, destroyed the wall and the Iron Curtain behind which the communist dictatorships had shut them. Round tables between ruling powers and "oppositions", especially in Poland, the opening of the Iron Curtain between Austria and Hungary in the spring, the Polish election of 4 June, the Hungarian communist party's change of name at the end of the year, and even the fall and execution of the Ceausescus in December paled into insignificance beside 9 November 1989. Even the Malta Summit of 2-3 December between U.S. President George H. Bush and Mikhail Gorbachev was eclipsed, even though it was the first between the two leaders and ended with declarations to the press suggesting that a new era was dawning. It is considered to be the last summit of the Cold War, despite the hackneyed, facile misnomer "from Yalta to Malta", since the Cold War did not start at the Yalta Conference. Although the repression in China in the spring of 1989 portrayed the country as lagging "behind" history, 1989 saw the normalisation of Sino-Soviet relations as well as the withdrawal of Vietnamese troops from Cambodia and the beginnings of the international negotiating process on Cambodia's future.[6]

Several members of the Reagan Administration, including one Jack Matlock, Special Assistant to the President and Senior Director of European and Soviet Affairs, subsequently U.S. Ambassador to the Soviet Union, considered the Cold War to be over at the end of the second term in 1988. The two countries no longer appeared to be enemies, particularly following Reagan's visit to Moscow in May. An ambitious disarmament treaty was signed (on intermediate-range missiles in 1987) and negotiations were underway on other agreements. In December, Gorbachev gave a much-acclaimed address to the United Nations Assembly: his announcements of unilateral disarmament measures and the de-ideologisation of Soviet foreign policy were received as paving the way for a peaceful Europe. 1988 saw the signature of the two agreements that led to the end of the Cold War in southern Africa and the Horn of Africa, and Moscow's announcement of the withdrawal of the Red Army from Afghanistan, completed by the beginning of the following year.[7]

Nevertheless, President Bush, who took up office in the White House in January 1989, and his team considered the Cold War to be far from over. It was not until the spring of 1990 that he redefined the enemy as instability.[8] In his speech to

---

[6] On the chronology of the Cold War in Asia, see Pierre Grosser, *L'histoire du monde se fait en Asie. Une autre histoire du XXe siècle*, Paris, Odile Jacob, 2e ed. 2019 and Lorenz Lüthi, *Cold Wars. Asia, Middle East, Europe, Cambridge*, Cambridge University Press, 2020.

[7] Flavia Gasbarri, *US Foreign Policy and the End of the Cold War in Africa. A Bridge between Global Conflict and the New World Order*, New York, Routledge, 2020, Artemy Kalinovsky, *A Long Goodbye: The Soviet Withdrawal from Afghanistan*, Cambridge (Mass.), Harvard University Press, 2011.

[8] Jeffrey A. Engel, *"When George Bush believed the Cold War ended and why that mattered"*, In: Michael Nelson and Barbara A. Perry (eds.) *41. Inside the Presidency of George H.W. Bush*, Ithaca, Cornell University Press, 2014.

Congress on 11 September 1990, he employed the term "new world order"; an expression conceived in early 1990 by his National Security Advisor Brent Scowcroft (who died in 2020). The term caused a lot of ink to flow, but vanished from the administration's rhetoric after the spring of 1991.[9]

In fact, it was rather 1990 that marked the end of the Cold War. 1989 ended on a note of real uncertainty as to the future of Eastern Europe's communist regimes, the future of Germany, what lay ahead for the Soviet Union and what was in store for Gorbachev.[10] In 1990, the communist parties and regimes disappeared from Eastern Europe. Washington took Moscow's acceptance of Germany's reunification inside NATO as evidence that the Cold War was over. And this is the option that won out in the bilateral meetings between Bush and Kohl, Bush and Gorbachev, and Kohl and Gorbachev from February to July of that year. These bilaterals carried more weight than the 12 September Two Plus Four Treaty (plus five in some measure, since Poland was in attendance for the issues that concerned it so as not to appear to reproduce the Yalta Conference). The quadripartism of 1945 (initially conceived as tripartism, without France, in 1943) had hence been revived to put an end to the Yalta-Potsdam system of four-handed management of the German question. On 1 October, all four countries relinquished their rights.[11] At the stroke of midnight on 3 October 1990, Germany was one again. The German-Soviet friendship and cooperation treaty was signed on 9 November, followed by the German-Polish Border Treaty (November) and then the Polish-German Treaty of Good Neighbourship and Friendly Cooperation (June 1991). It was not only the Cold War that was coming to an end, but the Second World War in Europe, since Germany had not been subject to the same peace treaties as its allies in Paris in 1947. In his press conference on 21 November 1990, Mitterrand even explained that the 1990 "road" put an end "to the state of insecurity created in Europe with, to put it simply, the advent of Hitler in Germany or, to put it more clearly, the Anschluss and Munich and then the war. Since this time, Europe has known no rest." Now, only Russia and Japan had not signed their peace treaty. So behind the French foreign office's spin on the event, the Paris Summit of 19-21 November was "just a formality", as historian Frédéric Bozo writes, since "everything was settled" for German reunification.[12] Gorbachev, crowned with his Nobel Prize announced in October, appeared as the star of the show when he was actually under siege in his own country.[13]

---

[9] Bartholomew Sparrow. *The Strategist: Brent Scowcroft and the Call of National Security*, New York, Public Affairs, 2015, Chapter 27.

[10] Joachim von Puttkamer, Wlodzimierz Borodziej and Stanislav Holubec (eds.) *From Revolution to Uncertainty. The Year 1990 in Central and Eastern Europe*, New York, Routledge, 2019.

[11] Georges-Henri Soutou, *La guerre de cinquante ans, Les relations Est-Ouest, 1943-1990*, Paris, Fayard, 2001.

[12] Frédéric Bozo, *Mitterrand, the End of the Cold War, and German Unification*, Oxford/New York, Berghahn Books, 2009, 450 p., translated by Susan Emanuel.

[13] William Taubman, *Gorbachev. His Life and Times*, New York, Simon & Schuster, 2017, Chapter 15.

Presentation of the Treaty of Moscow of 12 September 1990 on German reunification to the inhabitants of Halle, September 1990.

Although the START Treaty had to wait until the summer of 1991, the Treaty on Conventional Armed Forces in Europe was signed by 22 countries, also in Paris, in November 1990, after just 18 months of fast-track negotiations, albeit following 15 year of discussions. Soviet superiority on the continent, which had justified Western policy in the West, was now defunct. The London Declaration of 5 July, following the NATO meeting on transforming the North Atlantic Alliance, promised a change of military position and doctrine and enhancement of its political component, among other things to convince Moscow to accept Germany's reunification inside NATO. At the Rome Summit in November 1991, NATO effectively became more of a collective security organisation than a collective territorial defence organisation, although still under U.S. leadership. In March 1990, the Soviet Union announced the withdrawal of its forces from Eastern Europe; the process would take until 1994 to complete despite the Warsaw Pact being dissolved in July 1991.

Meanwhile, Iraq's invasion of Kuwait on 2 August 1990 turned all heads toward the Middle East. At the Paris Summit in November 1990, President Bush used the bilaterals with Gorbachev to discuss Iraq with him. The joint statement issued on 3 August by U.S. Secretary of State James Baker and Shevardnadze to condemn the invasion followed by Moscow's vote for UN Security Council Resolution 678 authorising the liberation of Kuwait by force showed that the page had finally turned on the vetoes and American-Soviet tensions at the UN. Baker was now positive that the Cold War was over. In actual fact, Bush's thinking was essentially that there was now only one superpower and that Moscow had no choice but to align its policy with that superpower, which is quite another approach to the end of the Cold War.[14] The Kremlin's use of force in the Baltic States in January 1991, on the eve of the expiry of the UN's ultimatum to Iraq, was not seen by the West as a "new Budapest" taking advantage of a "new Suez", as in the autumn of 1956: there was consequently neither concern nor a change of policy toward Moscow. The Cold War was already dead.[15] Precisely at the moment when the CSCE experts were meeting in Valletta in January 1991 to discuss the peaceful settlement of disputes, Desert Storm was getting underway and commanding the attention of the media and the international community.

And so the break-up of the Soviet Union on 26 December 1991 came after the end of the Cold War. Gorbachev had been invited to the G7 Summit at Lancaster House in July. In a televised address on 27 September, President Bush had spoken of "peace dividends" to justify a decrease in defence spending, the reduction in the U.S. strategic forces' alert level, and the end of the deployment of tactical nuclear forces. On 26 December, following Gorbachev's resignation, he addressed his fellow countrymen: "That [East-West] confrontation is now over. Eastern Europe is free. The Soviet Union itself is no more. This is a victory for democracy and freedom. It's a victory for the moral force of our values."[16]

- **Resituating the Charter of Paris in the shifting interpretations of the end of the Cold War**

The tone of this address reflected the intentional triumphalism in the United States' rhetoric. Bush's 1992 presidential campaign gave this rhetoric lasting momentum. The offensive strategies of the first Reagan administration and all those

---

[14] Jeffrey Engel, *When the World Seemed New. George W. Bush and the End of the Cold War*, New York, Houghton Mifflin Hancourt, 2017, Chapter 21.

[15] Una Bergmane, *"'Is this the End of Perestroïka?' International Reactions to the Use of Force in the Baltic Republics in January 1991"*, Journal of Cold War Studies, 2020, Vol. 22, No. 2.

[16] "End of the Soviet Union: Test of Bush's Address to the Nation on Gorbachev's Resignation", *The New York Times*, 26 December 1991.

who had fought communism in Europe appeared to have paid off.[17] In the late 1990s, the neoconservatives returned centre stage to tackle the "rogue states", asserting their role in the design and implementation of these strategies vis-à-vis the Soviet Union. Bush administration veterans vaunted their remarkable handling of the end of the Cold War, which had succeeded in achieving a "Europe whole and free" and a Germany reunified inside NATO.[18] Liberal internationalists admired how the United States had handled the victory, as they had after 1945 when they agreed to restrain their power within international organisations beneficial for all states.[19] In Europe, at the time, the tendency was rather to censure leaders who would swim against the tide of history, especially German reunification (first and foremost François Mitterrand and Margaret Thatcher), roll out another triumphalist, albeit divisive, narrative on the leap towards European unification (Maastricht Treaty and Economic and Monetary Union), and bemoan the powerlessness of Europe and its institutions to handle the wars triggered by the implosion of Yugoslavia and the conflicts on Russia's doorstep (Caucasia and Moldova) without U.S. leadership. In Germany, the triumphalist narrative somewhat trivialised the 1989-1990 sequence of events as merely the end of the totalitarian interlude, proving that the country clearly had another "liberal", "normal" history.[20] The history of the Cold War started to get lost in a teleological history of the progress of democracy, human rights and global governance, independent of geopolitics.

George W. Bush's presidency, and particularly the war in Iraq and its counter-insurgency quagmire, changed perceptions, as did the 2007-2008 turning point in relations with Russia (Putin's Munich address in February 2007 and the 2008 Russo-Georgian war), the rise of "populism" in Eastern Europe and the 2008 economic crisis. The war in Iraq sparked a transatlantic crisis, with "Old Europe" accused of being "from Venus" while the United States was "from Mars". It was in this climate that the focus sharpened on the role of the Europeans in the history of the Cold War: on the central role of Helmut Kohl, no longer in power since 1998; on the role of François Mitterrand, who not only was not opposed to German reunification, but was influential in the diplomatic process in the period from 1989 to 1991; on the

---

[17] On the first debates, see Pierre Grosser, *Les temps de la guerre froide. Réflexions sur l'histoire de la guerre froide et les causes de sa fin*, Bruxelles, Complexe, 1995.

[18] Philip Zelikow and Condoleeza Rice, *German Unified and Europe Transformed: A Study in Statecraft*, Cambridge (Mass.), Harvard University Press, 1995, George Bush and Brent Scowcroft, *A World Transformed. The Collapse of the Soviet Empire, the Unification of Germany, Tiananmen Square, The Gulf War*, New York, Knopf, 1998,

[19] G. John Ikenberry, *After Victory. Institutions, Strategic Restraint, and the Rebuilding of Order after Major Wars*, Princeton, Princeton University Press, 2001.

[20] On this narrative, see Jennifer L., Allen, "Against the 1989-1990 Ending Myth", *Central European History*, 2019, No. 52(1).

role of Margaret Thatcher, with the early opening of her archives; on the role of Austria in the fall of the Iron Curtain; and, more broadly, on the role of the "neutrals" throughout the entire period.[21] Eastern Europe historians argue that the leading powers, and the United States in particular, held back the 1989 emancipation processes for fear of jeopardising a Cold War system that was to their advantage, and that it was the small countries in the region, and especially their peoples, that changed history. The effect of this has been to partially "de-Americanise" the history of the end of the Cold War.

Secondly, with talk of a "new cold war", historians and practitioners looked back over the 1989-1991 sequence of events, wondering if there had not been a missed opportunity to bring Russia more on board in the new European order. A heated debate has been raging for 15 years over whether or not the United States and Germany gave Gorbachev assurances that NATO would not expand to the East — when expand it did in 1999, 2004 and 2009.[22] The other debate concerns the alternatives available at the time: the NATO and EU "prefabricated" institutions are said to have been imposed on the East, side-lining the ambitious pan-European proposals that included the transformation of the CSCE.[23] The missed opportunity assertion also holds that the CSCE, far from being invented as a Western weapon of war against the Soviet bloc (in particular by passing on the human rights bug), was first of all a Soviet proposal (there was one for Asia too), that the political will for a "common European home" was sincere and a lodestone in all the discussions on Europe, and that the West disregarded and denied this still-living tradition in order to marginalise Russia.[24] So political scientists now saw in the Bush administration a firm purpose, in the absence of a threat, to take advantage of the weakening of Soviet power in order to make optimum gains in the Third World and Europe, and to denigrate and exclude a Soviet Union that it refused to help economically.[25]

---

[21] Frédéric Bozo, *Mitterrand, the End of the Cold War, and German Unification, op. cit.*, Frédéric Bozo et al. (eds.), *Europe and the End of the Cold War: A Reappraisal*, London, Routledge, 2008; this watershed is starting to emerge in the historiography in the United States: Sarah Snyder "The Changing History of the End of the Cold War", In: Christian Dietrich. (Ed.) *A Companion to U.S. Foreign Relations*, Wiley, 2020.

[22] Among the historians, the debate was really launched by Mark Kramer, "The Myth of a No-NATO-Enlargement Pledge to Russia", *The Washington Quarterly*, 2009, Vol. 39, No. 2, and Mary E. Sarotte, "A Broken Promise? What the West Really Told Moscow About NATO Expansion?", *Foreign Affairs*, September-October 2014.

[23] Mary E. Sarotte, *1989. The Struggle to Create Post-Cold War Europe*, Princeton, Princeton University Press, 2009.

[24] Lauren Cramp, "A missed opportunity for a new Europe? The end of the Cold War and its consequences for Western European relations with Russia", In: Eleni Braat and Pepijn Corduwener (eds.) *1989 and the West. Western Europe since the end of the Cold War*, London, Routledge, 2020.

[25] Joshua R. Izkowitz Shifrinson, *Failing Giants. How Great Powers Exploit Power Shifts*, Ithaca, Cornell University Press, 2018 and "Eastbound and down: The United States, NATO enlargement, and sup-

A third shift was much less of an indictment of Bush senior's administration. Bush junior's policy, which appeared to have inherited the arrogance of Reagan's, became a foil for the United States. As a result, it was the policy of the second Reagan administration, which had extended a hand to the Soviets, that was held up during Obama's first term of office. Obama himself made reference to it to justify talks with Iran.[26] The "leap-to-trust" between Reagan and Gorbachev was seen as extraordinary and a model for conflict resolution.[27] With the impression of irresoluteness given by Obama (especially on Syria) and the election of the truculent Donald Trump in 2016, the diplomacy professionals, and especially those associated with the Bush senior administration, really pressed home the clarity of vision and method seen as being behind the successes of 1990.[28] In addition to these lessons in the exercise of power, it was even felt important once more to show that U.S. leadership accomplishes great things, particularly in Europe, especially given that the alternatives proposed by Gorbachev, such as the common European home, were, in their view, "nebulous" if not quite simply a trap.[29]

These shifts converged to retrace the history of the Charter of Paris. For France and its De Gaulle-Mitterrand legacy, it is important to show that the Mitterrand presidency conceived the inclusive security structures credited with preventing a new cold war and a new form of sharing the continent. Yalta, "the world carve-up in the absence of France", is part of Gaullist legend. Mitterrand wanted Europe to "cast off Yalta" and thought this was possible in the 1980s. "Yalta, which has become a symbol of the separation of Europe into different areas of influence, Yalta is over this very day in Paris," declared François Mitterrand at the press conference he held at the Élysée Palace following the signature of the Charter of Paris. The charter was meant to establish a post-Yalta (1945-1990) and pre-Sarajevo (1914) pan-European order. The handling of German reunification within NATO by talks between

---

pressing the Soviet and Western European alternatives, 1990-1992", forthcoming in *The Journal of Strategic Studies*, Kyle M. Lascurettes, *Orders of Exclusion. Great Powers and the Strategic Sources of Foundational Rules in International Relations*, New York, Oxford University Press, 2020.

[26] On the lessons learned from the end of the Cold War to the turn of the 2000s-2010s, see Pierre Grosser, *Traiter avec le diable ? Les vrais défis de la diplomatie au XXIe siècle*, Paris, Odile Jacob, 2013, Part I.

[27] Nicholas J. Wheeler, *Trusting Enemies: Interpersonal Relationships in International Conflict*, Oxford, Oxford University Press, 2018.

[28] Robert Hutchins, "American Diplomacy and the End of the Cold War in Europe", In Robert Hutchins and Jeremi Suri (eds.) *Foreign Policy Breakthroughs. Cases of Successful Diplomacy*, New York, Oxford University Press, 2015, Philip Zelikow and Condoleezza Rice, *To Build a Better World: Choices to End the cold War and Create a Global Commonwealth*, New York, Twelve, 2019.

[29] Kristina Spohr, *Post Wall, Post Square. Rebuilding the World Order*, New York, William Collins, 2019.

Washington, Bonn and Moscow – with France only having a secondary role – became a new form of Yalta (even though the United States, not the Soviet Union, was seen as the new winner of these talks), with similar repercussions in terms of tensions on the continent, which could have been avoided. It was for France to again propose, as it had back in the 1960s, a new pan-European vision, especially since the United States was once again suspected of being more interested in Asia than in Europe (in a parallel with the Vietnam War) and of concentrating on their domestic tensions and the negative consequences of their foreign interventions hither and thither (parallel with the 1970s).

Several East-Central European states, especially "small" countries that were neutral during the Cold War and were now concerned about growing tensions with Russia, reviewed their important role in the process leading to the Charter of Paris, here again seen as a missed opportunity to create a stable (since inclusive) security architecture.[30] So the Charter may well not be a virtually forgotten document from the past, but a seminal document to be put firmly back on the table and finally brought to life, thirty years on.

However, the 30th anniversary of 1989 revealed a fourth set of shifts, each with either a moderate or a radical face. First of all, 1989-1991 was portrayed as the moment when the United States was overcome with hubris, intent on changing the world and being its global policeman. "Realists" consequently criticised this sequence of events and, in particular, the choices made with respect to NATO and its expansion. As in the 1970s, an isolationist right faced an anti-imperialist left, itself repudiating the triumphalist narrative on 1989. This was then attacked by the left worldwide. The "triumph of freedom" was accused of being part of a counter-revolutionary cycle that started in the late 1970s: the events of 1989-1991, following on from the victory over the South and its will for a New International Economic Order, were a triumph for aggressive neoliberalism. With socialism and East-South anti-imperialist solidarities discredited, this strident neoliberalism allegedly took hold everywhere with the collusion of the elites and the international organisations and the support of American interventions. The growth in inequalities, false formal democracy and the militarisation of the forces of order inevitably sparked a resurgence of protests and revolutionary volition. Last but not least, it is argued that imported/exported foreign models, the opening of borders and the forms of imperialism practised by the United States, the European Union and the international organisations after 1989, especially in post-communist Eastern Europe, triggered "counter-revolutionary" reactions to the 1989 "models" in the name of national particularities and scorned "traditional" values.

---

[30] Christian Nünlist (ed.), *The Road to the Charter of Paris. Historical Narratives and Lessons for the OSCE today*, OSCE Network of Think Tanks and Academic Institutions, 2018: https://osce-network.net/file-OSCE-Network/Publications/Road_to_the_Charter_of_Paris_final_report.pdf

The return of debate surrounding the Charter of Paris consequently shows that the debates on the nature of the Cold War, the date and causes of its end, and especially its significance and the significance of the "post-Cold War" decades that followed, are far from over.

Frédéric BOZO
MITTERRAND'S VISION AND THE END OF THE COLD WAR

France's role and President François Mitterrand's personal record at the end of the Cold War have been widely debated since the events of 1989-91. It is often affirmed in the dominant literature that the part France played in that period was limited in comparison with that of other key actors, foremost the United States, the USSR, and Germany. Most accounts maintain that the French president essentially failed to anticipate the chain of events that led to the overcoming of the East-West conflict, namely the peaceful liberation of Eastern Europe, the unification of Germany and the breakup of the Soviet Union. It is generally assumed that Mitterrand's France was caught off guard by the acceleration of history' in the late 1980s and early 1990s and, worse yet, reacted obstructively to it. Paris allegedly tried to slow down or impede these events outright, especially German unification.[1]

This rendering of French policy at the end of the Cold War is intriguing. It is, to begin with, at odds with the role which French diplomacy, ever since the 1960s, had claimed under the impulse of General Charles de Gaulle: that of a challenger to the bloc system and Yalta'. Moreover, it contrasts with Mitterrand's adherence to the Gaullist legacy in foreign policy even before his coming to power in 1981 and his willingness, once elected president, to carry on a policy of overcoming the Cold War status quo. Finally, it contradicts what we now know of France's actual role in the events of 1989-91 thanks to archive-based research, a role that was, by and large, in accordance with the Gaullist (and the Mitterrandian) vision of overcoming the Cold War.[2]

It is therefore worth exploring what that vision was, before the revolutionary years 1989-91 provided the ultimate test of its validity, and evaluating how it met that test. The first section sketches out Mitterrand's concept of the end of the Cold

---

[1] For a general discussion, see F. Bozo. 2007. "Mitterrand's France, the end of the Cold War and German unification: a reappraisal", *Cold War History*, 7(4), 455-478.

[2] See F. Bozo. 2005. *Mitterrand, la fin de la guerre froide et l'unification allemande. De Yalta à Maastricht* Paris: Odile Jacob. (Published in English as *Mitterrand, The End of the Cold War, and German Unification*, New York: Berghahn, 2009.)

War in the early years of his presidency. His vision, in line with de Gaulle's, was one of overcoming "Yalta" as a long term objective. While this seemed a somewhat rhetorical aspiration as the "new" Cold War was culminating in the early 1980s, Gorbachev's coming to power in 1985 gave it renewed credence. The second section looks at Mitterrand's vision on the eve of the dramatic events of the autumn of 1989. With the confirmation of Gorbachev's readiness to break with past Soviet policies, especially starting in 1988, ending the Cold War became a more concrete possibility, at least in the medium term. By 1989, it is fair to say that Mitterrand, perhaps more than other Western leaders, had a clear vision of how to overcome "Yalta". The final section looks at the confrontation between Mitterrand's vision of a progressive ending of the East-West conflict and the "acceleration of history" that occurred in 1989-91. While there is no denying that the actual unfolding of the end of the Cold War did not match earlier French anticipations and preferences, the vision was eventually reconciled with the reality.

- **De Gaulle, Mitterrand, and "Overcoming Yalta"**

It would be impossible to explain Mitterrand's concept for overcoming the Cold War in the 1980s without taking into account the enduring influence of the Gaullist legacy. In the 1960s, President Charles de Gaulle had been the first Western statesman to articulate a far-reaching (and in many ways dissident) vision of going beyond the East-West conflict. At a time when the dominant Western approach postulated that the end of the Cold War would result from a preponderance of the West over the East, de Gaulle's central premise was that the Cold War stalemate – "Yalta" in de Gaulle's parlance - could only be overcome by calling into question the very logic of "blocs". This presupposed the USSR's progressive abandonment of coercion in the East and confrontation with the West (a scenario that by the mid-1960s seemed plausible in de Gaulle's eyes, at least in the medium term) as well as the gradual withdrawal of the U.S. from the continent (which he believed to be unavoidable in the long term). Meanwhile, the strengthening of European unity, which would lead to the emergence of a Western Europe more autonomous from the U.S. (and therefore in a better position to intensify relations with the East and the Soviet Union), would stimulate the softening of the Soviet grip and the emancipation of Eastern Europe. Eventually, these evolutions would allow for the emergence of a "greater Europe" stretching "from the Atlantic to the Urals" and free of the divisions imposed by the Cold War, leading to a pan-European settlement with a reunified Germany at its core – an outcome, he reckoned, that would require a "generation".[3]

---

[3] For an analysis of de Gaulle's Cold War policies and post-Cold War vision, see F. Bozo. 2010. "France, 'Gaullism', and the Cold War", in M. P. Leffler and O. A. Westad (eds.), *Cambridge History of the Cold War*, vol. 2, Cambridge: Cambridge University Press, 2010.

MITTERRAND'S VISION AND THE END OF THE COLD WAR

In spite of the brutal confirmation of the East-West status quo that took place in the wake of the 1968 Soviet-led invasion of Czechoslovakia, the Gaullist vision had essentially remained at the core of French diplomacy ever since. By the time of his election in May 1981, Mitterrand – although a socialist and a longtime opponent of de Gaulle – had all but espoused it: "All that contributes to the exit from Yalta is good", he declared typically on New Year's Eve 1982.[4] His long term expectations were in line with the de Gaulle's, in particular with regard to evolutions in the East. He later reported that after his election he had instructed his staff to "articulate our foreign policy conceptions around a major hypothesis: by 2000, the Soviet empire would be over".[5] The "Soviet empire" would be critically weakened within "fifteen years", he confided to a sceptical West German Chancellor Helmut Schmidt in the autumn of 1981, adding (like de Gaulle) that this would make a German reunification possible within a "generation".[6] Regarding Eastern Europe, the Elysée was convinced as early as 1981 that the Soviet grip was now weakened and that the popular democracies would eventually become, as it were, "Finlandized".[7] "A national liberal trend is developing" there, Mitterrand told U.S. President Ronald Reagan three years later.[8]

So how could one exploit these underlying trends and overcome "Yalta"? Mitterrand's approach, here also, was a continuation of that of de Gaulle and his successors. The French president saw the pursuit of European integration and the build-up of a more autonomous Western Europe as the most powerful lever to move beyond the status quo: "If we manage to give Europe a political will", he told the newly elected chancellor Helmut Kohl in 1982 (with whom he would quickly establish a close personal relationship), "we will have accomplished a historic task".[9] And although it was for him a matter of lesser urgency, Mitterrand saw the pursuit of the pan-European process as an important component of the strategy to overcome the logic of blocs: "Helsinki", it was thought in the Elysée, was an avenue that could well lead, in the long run, to an "exit from Yalta".[10]

Yet in the early 1980s all this seemed quite distant. With the "new" Cold War culminating in those years (as the Euromissile crisis, Afghanistan and Poland loomed

---

[4] Mitterrand's New Year address, 31 Dec. 1981, *Politique étrangère de la France*, Nov.-Dec. 1981, 85.
[5] F. Mitterrand. 1996. *De l'Allemagne, de la France*, Paris: Odile Jacob, 12-13.
[6] Minutes of the meeting between Mitterrand and Schmidt, Latché, 7 Oct. 1981, private papers.
[7] Jean-Michel Gaillard, handwritten note for Hubert Védrine, undated (May 1981), Archives nationales (AN), 5AG4/11386.
[8] Minutes of the meeting between Mitterrand and Reagan, Washington, 22 and 23 Mar. 1984, private papers.
[9] Minutes of the meeting between Mitterrand and Kohl, Paris, 14 Oct. 1982, private papers.
[10] Pierre Morel, note pour Monsieur le Président, "Le sommet de Versailles, le sommet de Bonn et les relations Est-Ouest", 1 June 1982, AN, 5AG4/2266.

in the background), the objective of ending the East-West confrontation, let alone of overcoming the Iron Curtain, was a long term goal at best. Mitterrand, in fact, had initially pursued tough policies towards the East, as illustrated by his famous January 1983 Bundestag speech on Intermediate Nuclear Forces (INF). Still, if an exit from the Cold War in the wider sense was a speculative scenario early in the decade, Mitterrand soon proved eager to overcome the "new" Cold War. His aim, starting in 1983-84, was to restore an East-West climate more conducive to France's long term goals. One should be ready to resume dialogue with the Soviets "on the inevitable day when [they] want to discuss things", he told President Reagan in March 1984 before going to Moscow.[11]

The coming to power of Mikhail Gorbachev one year later was a turning point. "The Soviet Union might at long last exit from its immobility", the Elysée now hoped.[12] To be sure, Mitterrand was at first under no illusions as to the profound consequences of the change of leadership in Moscow on Soviet policies, let alone on the very structure of the Cold War system, at least in the foreseeable future. Gorbachev's coming to power, he told his ministers after his first encounter with the new secretary general in March 1985, marked a generational change and "the passage from one era to another"; but, he added, although the Soviet leader has shown himself "charming and smiling", this did not mean he would "renounce" past Soviet policies.[13] Still, because it heralded less confrontational policies and a more serene East-West climate, Gorbachev'advent offered Mitterrand an opportunity to return to a more actively Gaullist foreign policy and to emphasize long-term aims again. "If new possibilities of a modus vivendi with the Soviet Union open up this would be a good thing", he told Gorbachev during his October 1985 visit to France (his first foreign trip as secretary general), stressing that strengthening Western Europe' was for him a major perspective that Moscow should welcome.[14]

The French president then sketched out a long-term vision of East-West relations: "There is a situation in Europe inherited from the war", he recognized, but one might "correct" this situation by "expanding" relations between Eastern Europe and Western Europe, he affirmed, encouraging the Soviets to "take the hand" of the European Community (EC).[15] Shortly after Gorbachev's visit, he made a lyrical public presentation of his East-West concept: "We are living in the era of Yalta", he said,

---

[11] Minutes of the meeting between Mitterrand and Reagan, Washington, 22 and 23 Mar. 1984, private papers.

[12] Hubert Védrine, note pour le président de la République, "Obsèques de M. Tchernenko", 12 Mar. 1985, private papers.

[13] Record of the council of ministers, 14 Mar. 1985, private papers.

[14] Minutes of the meeting between Mitterrand and Gorbachev, Paris, 2 Oct. 1985, private papers.

[15] Minutes of the meeting between Mitterrand and Gorbachev, Paris, 4 Oct. 1985, private papers.

but this situation is not satisfactory. "[T]he gradual affirmation of Western Europe's autonomous personality, the promotion of its complementarities with Eastern Europe, the obligation of the USSR to re-establish a more trusting climate with Community countries in order to stimulate its exchanges and to foster its development", he maintained, "all this will slowly displace the immobile horizon of the last forty years" and give rise to "awareness after a half century of ignorance of [our] belonging to the same continent, expressing the same civilization", thus hastening "the hour of Europe, the true Europe, that of history and of geography".[16]

During the three years that followed the advent of Gorbachev, this scenario for overcoming the Cold War nevertheless remained by and large what it had been since de Gaulle, i.e. a long-term vision. By 1988 however, its main premise – the Soviet Union's profound evolution – was beginning to gain credence. Hence, in the wake of his reelection to a second presidential term in the spring, Mitterrand decided to vigorously revive France's dormant *politique à l'Est* through a series of high-profile visits to Eastern countries, a decision that was predicated on his belief that Moscow had now renounced the use of force in Eastern Europe.[17] Political developments in Moscow confirmed Mitterrand's intuition. The nineteenth Communist Party of the Soviet Union (CPSU) conference in June and the changes that Gorbachev imposed within the party apparatus over the summer considerably reinforced his internal power, allowing him to make a quantum leap in his "New Thinking". By autumn, French diplomacy believed that the USSR had in effect renounced a "messianic" foreign policy based on class struggle applied to international relations in favour of the search for "the common interests of all mankind".[18] As seen from Paris, Gorbachev's speech at the United Nations in December 1988 confirmed this, marking a clean break with the "revolutionary" inspiration of Soviet policy.[19] (Gorbachev's entourage agreed: "Your UN speech", Anatoly Chernyaev wrote to him, "brought us to a new level in world politics. Now we can't afford concessions to the policies of the past."[20]) The changes in Soviet policy in the last months of 1988 were so dramatic that by the early weeks of 1989, French diplomats believed that a forty-year status quo was now in effect drawing to an end. "Everyone feels", wrote the Quai d'Orsay

---

[16] F. Mitterrand. 1986. *Réflexions sur la politique étrangère de la France*, Paris: Fayard.

[17] P. Favier and M. Martin Roland. 1996. *La Décennie Mitterrand*, vol. 3, Paris: Seuil, 167.

[18] Ministère des affaires étrangères (MAE), Centre d'analyse et de prévision, note, "Entretiens de planification franco-soviétiques", 29 Sept. 1988, Archives diplomatiques (AD), Europe 1986-1990, URSS, box 6674.

[19] MAE, Sous-direction d'Europe orientale, note, "Discours de M. Gorbatchev devant l'AGNU", 7 Dec. 1988, AD, Europe 1986-1990, URSS, box 6649.

[20] A. S. Chernyaev. 2000. *My Six Years with Gorbachev*, University Park: Pennsylvania University Press, 148.

political director, "that the organization of Europe born of the Second World War is being replaced by something new although we don't know clearly where we are going".[21] The time had come to effectively look beyond "Yalta".

• Before the Wall: Mitterrand's vision in 1989

By the early months of 1989, therefore, it was clear to President Mitterrand and French diplomacy that the Cold War was drawing to an end and that a new era was in the making. The Gaullist-Mitterrandian vision, in other words, was beginning to be validated by events. As a result, what had been, during the past twenty-five years or so, a long-term, hypothetical perspective was in essence becoming a medium-term, plausible scenario – although it was clearly not yet a short-term political reality. So what was Mitterrand's script for overcoming "Yalta" in the months preceding the dramatic events of the autumn of 1989? What were the French expectations or assumptions regarding the ongoing evolutions in the East? What were their preferred Western responses to these evolutions? And how, as seen from Paris, would East-West relations move from conflict to cooperation and to a new European order?[22]

More than ever, ending the Cold War was premised, in French eyes, on the continued transformation of Soviet policies. By early 1989, this seemed to be a safe bet. The Quai d'Orsay predicted that the evolutions that had been triggered in Moscow in 1988 would be "prolonged" and even "amplified" the following year.[23] This, in turn, made an acceleration of change in Eastern Europe likely. By spring 1989, the French believed that the old "status quo" had now been replaced by increased "*fluidity*" inside the Soviet sphere and that this tendency could but intensify in the near future.[24] Mitterrand's 1981 prediction seemed confirmed: "The Soviet empire", he assured U.S. President George H. W. Bush in May, will "unravel".[25] Yet Mitterrand's vision of the future evolution of Eastern Europe was not one of a radical rupture. Of course, by 1989 the French president was convinced that the end

---

[21] MAE, le directeur des affaires politiques (B. Dufourcq), note, "De l'Europe d'aujourd'hui à celle de demain", 20 Feb. 1989, AD, Directeur politique, box 305.

[22] For analysis of Mitterrand's vision on the eve of the dramatic events of 1989, see Bozo, *Mitterrand*, 94-102.

[23] MAE, Direction d'Europe, Le directeur adjoint, note, "Visite officielle de M. Qian Qichen", 3 Jan. 1989, AD, Europe 1986-1990, box 6097.

[24] MAE, Direction d'Europe, sous-direction d'Europe orientale, note, "L'URSS et ses alliés est-européens", 8 Mar. 1989, AD, Europe 1986-1990, box 6092.

[25] Minutes of the meeting between Mitterrand and Bush, Kennebunkport, 21 May 1989, private papers.

of "Yalta" would come about primarily as a result of the generalization of the democratic process already under way in countries like Hungary and Poland (which, he suggested, might become associate members in the Council of Europe).[26] But he also seemed to assume that in the foreseeable future these countries would remain somehow "socialist" in socio-economic terms and that they would wish one way or another to remain linked to the Soviet Union in geopolitical terms. This might take place within a revamped, "politicized" Warsaw Pact in which they would regain their full international sovereignty (by spring 1989, Gorbachev's all but complete refutation of the "Brezhnev doctrine" seemed to validate this scenario).[27] Poland, where Mitterrand paid a visit in mid-June – in between the two rounds of the first free elections held in that country since 1947 – seemed to offer the best illustration of what the French president considered the right mix between internal democratization and geopolitical continuity: the transition in Poland, Mitterrand told General Wojtech Jaruzelski, "took facts into account, but in order to change them".[28]

In 1989, the Mitterrandian vision of the future of East-West relations beyond "Yalta", therefore, was one of a smooth rapprochement between the two halves of the divided continent, and not one of a rapid and dramatic collapse of the post-1945 European order. In geopolitical terms, the Elysée wagered on a progressive effacement of the logic of military blocs (thanks in particular to the pursuit of disarmament), but not on a complete disappearance of the dividing line between the military alliances, at least in the short or medium term.[29] In political and socio-economic terms, the vision was also one of a progressive convergence between the two systems, with Eastern Europe steadily becoming more liberal democratic and Western Europe more social democratic: "The Eastern countries must make progress toward individual liberties", Mitterrand told the Hungarian leader Karoly Grosz in November 1988, "and the Western countries must make progress toward collective social liberties".[30] All this, the French believed, would make it possible to progressively overcome Europe's Cold War divisions in the years and decades to come. The transformations in Eastern Europe and, to begin with, the internal democratization of the former Soviet satellites and their political emancipation from Moscow, the Elysée anticipated, would help restore throughout the continent "a real fluidity both in political relations between states as well as in contacts of all kinds between individuals",

---

[26] Mitterrand's address on the fortieth anniversary of the Council of Europe, 5 May 1989, *Politique étrangère de la France*, May-June 1989, 8-11.

[27] On this see Bozo, *Mitterrand*, 95-96.

[28] Minutes of the meeting between Mitterrand and Jaruzelski, Warsaw, 14 June 1989, private papers.

[29] "Argumentaire à propos de la visite de François Mitterrrand en Tchécoslovaquie", Dec. 1988, private papers.

[30] Minutes of the meeting between Mitterrand and Grosz, Budapest, 18 Nov. 1988, private papers.

thereby helping to surmount in concrete terms the forty-year division of the continent.[31] Last but not least, these evolutions would create a European context more conducive to the emergence of a practical solution to the German problem. The intensification of rapprochement between East and West, French diplomats believed – a reasoning not unlike that which remained in the background of West Germany's Ostpolitik – would indeed open the way to rapprochement between the two Germanys, which would thus be able to "surmount if not the political division, then at least the human division from which the German people suffers".[32]

The Mitterrandian concept for the future evolution of European "architecture" beyond the Cold War was in accordance with the foregoing. On the pan-European level, the Helsinki process was of course seen as pivotal in the 1989 context. In the short or medium term, the director of political affairs at the Quai d'Orsay noted in the early weeks of the year, "The pan-European dimension will in all likelihood become more prominent".[33] The CSCE framework, Mitterrand confirmed in June 1989, was a necessity in order to "overcome the divisions that separate European nations and truly establish confidence among them".[34] Yet the CSCE was no panacea. Although it was seen as a useful framework in order to help assuage the logic of blocs thanks in particular to the linkages between its three baskets, French diplomacy remained somewhat fearful of a transformation of the CSCE into a pan-European collective security body, which had long been a traditional Soviet aim. Moreover, by 1989 the CSCE was seen as an inadequate framework for the intensified pan-European cooperation that Mitterrand wanted to encourage in areas such as energy, technology, or culture in order to overcome the East-West divide through concrete projects and promote a truly "European" Europe – i.e. a Europe free of the outside influence of the superpowers. "The Europe of which we might dream in the long term", his diplomatic adviser Hubert Védrine wrote in November 1988, was "a Europe at 32 (i.e., Western Europe without the U.S. and Canada plus Eastern Europe without Russia)".[35] One year before the fall of the Berlin Wall, in a context characterized by Gorbachev's propagation of his own "common home" concept, Mitterrand and his entourage were already thinking along the lines of what would become the "European confederation" proposal of December 31 1989.[36]

---

[31] "Argumentaire", Dec. 1988, private papers.
[32] MAE, le directeur des affaires politiques, note, "De l'Europe d'aujourd'hui", 20 Feb. 1989.
[33] MAE, le directeur des affaires politiques, note, "De l'Europe d'aujourd'hui", 20 Feb. 1989.
[34] Mitterrand interview with *Moscow News*, 1 June 1989, private papers.
[35] Hubert Védrine, note pour le président de la République, 19 Nov. 1988, private papers.
[36] On this see F. Bozo. 2008. "The failure of a grand design: Mitterrand's European confederation (1989-1991)", *Contemporary European History*, *17*(3), 391-412; and M.-P. Rey. 2004. "Europe is our Common Home: A Study of Gorbachev's Diplomatic Concept", *Cold War History*, *4*(2), 63-65.

Yet by 1989 the West European dimension was no doubt the dominant one in the French vision of European architecture beyond "Yalta". "The Twelve [EC member states]", noted Védrine typically, "are the best placed to conceive and implement... a regular, constant and smooth re-establishment of links between the two Europes".[37] For French diplomacy, it was up to the EC to foster the "gradual rapprochement" between Western and Eastern Europe and thus to serve "as magnet to the various parcels of a Soviet Empire on its way to being Ottomanized". The EC was also seen as the most appropriate framework for the gradual rapprochement between the two Germanys: "Managing the German problem", the Quai underlined, meant first of all "tying the Federal Republic strongly to the Community, with Franco-German relations being the privileged means" to that end.[38] Overall, therefore, a strong European Community appeared to Mitterrand's diplomacy on the eve of the events of the autumn as the key condition of a stable transition toward post-Cold War Europe. Inversely, the end of "Yalta" was perceived as an opportunity to make the EC the cornerstone of a Europe beyond blocs. "Pursuing the construction of the Europe of Twelve and working to re-establish the unity of our continent", in short, were "two projects that, far from being opposite, complement[ed] and reinforce[d] each other".[39] The bottom line was clear: as seen from Paris, the strengthening of the EC and of its cohesion had become "an absolute priority".[40]

Clearly, Mitterrand and his advisors saw the ongoing transition as a progressive, incremental process. Although the overcoming of "Yalta" had certainly become a shorter-term possibility in their vision than it had been years or even months before, the French did not visualize as rapid a departure from the status quo as would indeed take place in the autumn of 1989. This was, first of all, a predictive position. For French diplomats, the tendencies that would lead "from the Europe of today to that of tomorrow" were not likely to yield dramatic results, at least not immediately; rather, they had to be appraised in a "medium to long term" perspective, i.e. within a ten- to twenty-year period.[41] Mitterrand's own predictions were quite similar, in particular regarding the weakening of the Soviet Union and the intra-German rapprochement and their respective paces (in his view, those two processes were closely interrelated). Reiterating to Bush in May 1989 his conviction that the Soviet empire would sooner or later collapse and that this would make German unification possible, he estimated that these two events "would not happen in the next ten years" and he emphasized that "the USSR will not accept [German

---

[37] Hubert Védrine, note pour le président de la République, 6 Apr. 1989, private papers.
[38] MAE, le directeur des affaires politiques, note, "De l'Europe d'aujourd'hui", 20 Feb. 1989.
[39] MAE, dossier de synthèse, "a.s. Visite de M. Gorbatchev (4-6 juillet 1989)", AD, URSS, Europe 1986-1990, box 6685.
[40] MAE, le directeur des affaires politiques, note, "De l'Europe d'aujourd'hui", 20 Feb. 1989.
[41] MAE, le directeur des affaires politiques, note, "De l'Europe d'aujourd'hui", 20 Feb. 1989.

unification] as long as it remains strong".⁴² Yet this was also a prescriptive position. For Mitterrand's diplomacy, the end of the Cold War in Europe was indeed a desirable perspective, but it also carried the danger, if poorly managed, of a return of instability in the East, not least as a consequence of a return of ethnic conflict: "One may wish the desegregation of the [Soviet] empire, which should not last very long", he declared in July 1988, "but one may also fear the consequences".⁴³ By 1989, French diplomacy was both upbeat about the intensification of change in the East and wary of it gaining too much pace: "we have no interest in an excessive acceleration", the Quai d'Orsay believed.⁴⁴

- ### *The fall of the Wall and the "Acceleration of History"*

Yet, starting in the summer of 1989, a dramatic acceleration did occur. The GDR refugee crisis, which culminated in September, marked a turning point. To be sure, the French continued to believe in the validity of their scenario: the "extraordinary events" that were unfolding, Védrine wrote in September against the backdrop of the refugee crisis, announced "the progressive overcoming of Yalta" and the emergence of a "greater Europe" through a "continued and controlled evolution in the East". This evolution, he emphasized, was "in line with what has happened since 1985", i.e., since the advent of Gorbachev.⁴⁵ A month later, in spite of yet another and even more dramatic acceleration in the East signalled by the downfall of Erich Honecker on October 18, his analysis remained essentially in the same vein. True, Védrine wrote, events in East Berlin did confirm the "inevitability" of the ongoing rapprochement between the two Germanys, but this would in all likelihood remain an open-ended process both in terms of pace (it would take place step by step) and outcome (although the recreation of a single German state could not be ruled out in the end, other, intermediary solutions for unification were also conceivable). "Everything would remain manageable", Védrine believed, "if the process of ending the division of Germany [did] not go faster than the process of European construction and the overall abolition of barriers between Eastern Europe and Western Europe". European integration, therefore, had to be accelerated and be used as a "magnet" in order to stabilize Eastern Europe; meanwhile, the military alliances would continue to guarantee European stability for an "intermediary period" that

---

⁴² Minutes of the meeting between Mitterrand and Bush, Kennebunkport, 21 May 1989.
⁴³ Transcript of a meeting of the Defence council, 20 July 1988, private papers.
⁴⁴ MAE, le directeur des affaires politiques, note, "De l'Europe d'aujourd'hui", 20 Feb. 1989.
⁴⁵ Hubert Védrine, note pour le président de la République, 13 Sept. 1980, private papers.

could well prove to be "rather long". "The issue of the relative rhythms [of these processes]", Mitterrand's strategic advisor concluded pointedly, "is of the essence".[46]

Yet the fall of the Berlin Wall on November 9, 1989 – which of course no one had foreseen in Bonn, Washington, Moscow or Paris – shattered all previous assumptions and expectations. Until then, the French had believed that the evolutions in the East were essentially validating their preferred scenario for the end of the Cold War. Now, things were becoming unpredictable. Because of their suddenness and of their magnitude, events contradicted the anticipation of a step-by-step convergence between Europe's two halves that would require years if not decades, rather than the months or weeks, that indeed would be the case. Events simply no longer followed the script. Like all other diplomacies – but perhaps even more so, precisely because it had a well-written script – French diplomacy was caught off guard by what amounted to the eruption of the peoples on a scene once dominated by diplomats and statesmen: *"This is a phenomenal acceleration"*, the head of the European directorate at the Quai d'Orsay commented in the following days, speaking of a "reawakening of history".[47]

As seen from Paris, the fall of the Wall and the ensuing events challenged the heretofore privileged scenario for ending the Cold War in at least two important ways. First, the acceleration of events would – from the announcement of Kohl's ten-point plan for German unification in the Bundestag on November 28 1989 to Moscow's "green light" in late January 1990 – become even more "phenomenal", leading to a unified and sovereign Germany on October 3 1990, i.e., in barely 329 days, according to Horst Teltschik's famous reckoning.[48] This was hardly the kind of a "progressive" scenario that, until the late weeks of 1989, had been anticipated in Paris and elsewhere. Second, the "rush" toward German unity meant that contrary to earlier French predictions or preferences, the German and the wider European evolutions (meaning in particular West European integration and the pan-European process) would not be easily reconciled, with the former taking clear precedence over the latter. Mitterrand acknowledged as much in February 1990, confiding to the Italian Premier Giulio Andreotti that West European integration was but "a local train" in comparison with the "express train" of German unification.[49] The "relative rhythms" of German unification and Europe's transformation, as feared in Paris, had, in effect, diverged.

One week before the fall of the Berlin Wall, the French president, asked how he felt about the acceleration of events, famously responded that he did not "fear"

---

46   Hubert Védrine, note, "Réflexions sur la question allemande", 18 Oct. 1989, private papers.
47   MAE, note du directeur d'Europe, "Le réveil de l'histoire", 16 Nov. 1989, AN, 5AG4/7708.
48   See H. Teltschik. 1991. *329 Tage. Innenansichten der Einigung*, Berlin: Siedler.
49   Minutes of the meeting between Mitterrand and Andreotti, Paris, 13 Feb. 1990, private papers.

German unification: "I do not ask myself this kind of questions as history moves forward. History is there. I take it as it is", he said, adding that France would "adapt its policies" accordingly.[50] So how did Mitterrand's diplomacy "adapt" to the new situation in the critical months that followed the fall of the Wall? Clearly not by trying to slow down, let alone block German unification, as has often – and wrongly – been said.[51] Although the French president did not conceal his nervousness about what he considered to be Kohl's excessive precipitation with regard to German unification, he stuck to the line which he had announced publicly as early as July 1989: German unification was legitimate, provided it took place "peacefully and democratically".[52] "Whether I like it or not, unification is for me a historic reality which it would be unfair and foolish to oppose", he told Kohl in early January 1990, meanwhile recognizing that "if [I] were German, I would be in favour of as quick a reunification as possible".[53] Mitterrand fully understood that running against the course of history would destroy the achievement of four decades of Franco-German reconciliation and European unification. "I am not saying no to German reunification. This would be stupid and unrealistic", he told the British Prime Minister Margaret Thatcher at the end of January.[54]

Mitterrand's approach was in fact the opposite of Thatcher's. Rather than try to slow down unification, French diplomacy, in 1989-90, essentially strove to reconcile the European agenda with the German agenda. This was done in two ways. The first was to embed German unity within an international and a European framework in order to manage its geopolitical consequences and ensure its "pacific" and "democratic" character: while "the national consequences" of German unification were the business of the Germans, "the international consequences" had to be discussed in an international framework, Mitterrand told Kohl in February 1990.[55] To that effect, Paris sought to make the best of the "2+4" talks in spring and summer 1990, insisting in particular on the need to settle the German-Polish border issue as a prerequisite to German unification.[56] Most of all, Mitterrand's priority was to firmly

---

[50] Kohl-Mitterrand joint press conference, Bonn, 3 Nov. 1989, *Politique étrangère de la France*, Nov.-Dec. 1989, 4-6.
[51] For an archivally-based refutation of the narrative of France's opposition to German unification, see Bozo, *Mitterrand*, and "Mitterrand's France".
[52] Interview with five European newspapers, 27 July 1989, *Politique étrangère de la France*, Jul.-Aug. 1989, 78-82.
[53] Gespräch des Bundeskanzlers Kohl mit Staatspräsident Mitterrand, Latché, 4 Januar 1990, in H. J. Küsters and D. Hofmann (eds.). 1998. *Deutsche Einheit. Sonderedition aus den Akten des Bundeskanzleramtes 1989/90*, Munich: R. Oldenburg, 682-690.
[54] Minutes of the meeting between Mitterrand and Thatcher, 20 Jan. 1990, private papers.
[55] Gespräch des Bundeskanzlers Kohl mit Staatspräsident Mitterrand, Paris, 15 Februar 1990, in Küsters and Hofmann, *Deutsche Einheit*, 851-2.
[56] On this, see F. Bozo, *Mitterrand*, pp. 212 ff.

anchor a unified Germany in European and international institutions – particularly, in France's ascending order of preference, the CSCE, the Atlantic alliance and, above all, the European Community – a policy that culminated at the December 1989 European Council in Strasbourg, when the French president obtained the German chancellor's definitive acceptance of the Economic and Monetary Union (EMU) project and the insurance that a unified Germany would thus remain tightly integrated into the EC.[57]

Inversely, Mitterrand was determined to promote his vision of the post "Yalta" organization of the continent beyond German unification, a vision that of course had European integration at its core. This effort culminated, in the spring of 1990, in a fresh Franco-German impulse to relaunch European construction, leading to the signing of the Maastricht treaty some 18 months later. This was a direct consequence of German unification and of Mitterrand's and Kohl's determination to build on its momentum in order to promote their long-standing European objectives and to "face up to [their] joint responsibility with regard to European unification".[58] Maastricht was thus the endpoint of France's management of the transition toward a post-Cold War European order. It was, Mitterrand commented, "one of the most important events of the past half century" and one that "prepares the next century".[59]

To be sure, France's vision was only partially fulfilled in the following decade. The Maastricht treaty notwithstanding, Europe after "Yalta" was not – at least not yet – what the French had imagined and wished for. The failure of Mitterrand's European confederation project in spring 1991 was an illustration. Announced in December 1989, the project was premised on the anticipation that the convergence between the two halves of the divided continent would be progressive and that the post-Cold War order would be fixed around a Western Europe that would become its cornerstone. It collapsed because Eastern and Central European countries were now intent on joining Western institutions (European or Atlantic) as quickly as possible.[60] Another setback was the limited rebalancing of the transatlantic relationship that French diplomacy was able to obtain in the immediate aftermath of the end of the Cold War. The demise of the Soviet empire and indeed of the USSR did not

---

[57] On this, see F. Bozo. 2008a. "France, German unification, and European integration", in F. Bozo, M.-P. Rey, L. Nuti, and N.P. Ludlow (eds), *Europe and the End of the Cold War: A Reappraisal*, London: Routledge.

[58] J. Bitterlich. 1998. "In memoriam Werner Rouget. Frankreichs (und Europas) Weg nach Maastricht im Jahr der deutschen Einheit", in W. Rouget (ed.), *Schwierige Nachbarschaft am Rhein: Frankreich-Deutschland*, Bonn: Bouvier.

[59] Interview on TF1, 15 Dec. 1991, *Politique étrangère de la France*, Nov.-Dec. 1991, 151-8.

[60] On this see Bozo, "The failure of a grand design"; and V. Mastny. 2008. "Eastern Europe and the early prospects for EC/EU and NATO membership", in Bozo, Rey, et al. (eds), *Europe and the End of the Cold War*.

lead, at least immediately, to an American disengagement from the old continent, as anticipated since de Gaulle. Yet, in hindsight, the decisions made in 1989-91 eventually opened the way to the sort of post-Cold War Europe that had been envisaged in Paris since the 1960s. Since September 11 2001, the U.S. has effectively begun to disengage from the Old Continent. Meanwhile the European Union, now with twenty-seven member states, has emerged as the privileged framework for the reunification of Europe at large. In retrospect, then, those decisions – Maastricht to begin with – have laid the groundwork for today's Europe, in some ways vindicating the vision of a "European" Europe that had been at the centre of French diplomacy for decades.

Nicolas BADALASSI*
THE "*MAGNA CARTA* OF FREEDOM"
THE CHARTER OF PARIS IN THE HISTORY OF THE CSCE

The "*Magna Carta* of freedom" is how Helmut Kohl hailed the Charter of Paris for a New Europe following the Summit of the Conference on Security and Co-operation in Europe (CSCE) meeting on Avenue Kléber in the French capital on 19, 20 and 21 November 1990.[1] These words from the mouth of a Chancellor who could no longer be called "West German" since the previous month speak volumes about the symbolic value of this document signed by 34 Heads of State and Government of Europe and North America. They show how the spirit of the CSCE was in perfect tune with the prevailing spirit of the 1989 revolutions, just as the bloc mentality became a thing of the past. The conference was seen as the most appropriate multilateral instrument to coordinate the transformation of Europe, especially since its composition made it the only forum representative of both "Greater Europe" and "transatlantic Europe".[2]

Yet this purpose called for changes to the CSCE's provisions, objectives and procedures. Such were the main challenges in the months leading up to the signature of the Charter of Paris: the preparatory negotiations held in Vienna from July to November 1990, in the midst of a dizzying chain of events, were tasked with a rethink of the CSCE's architecture in a move to establish the conference as a benchmark tool in the post-Cold War era. The Charter of Paris was hence built on teamwork and collective thinking, which augured well for an overhaul of international practices driven by the multilateralization movement that had got underway in the last two decades of the Cold War. Yet what precisely did the Charter of Paris provide

---

[*] Aix-en-Provence Institute of Political Studies.
[1] Helmut Kohl, *Regierungserklärung zu den Ergebnissen des Gipfeltreffens der Staats- und Regierungschefs der KSZE in Paris und zum Europäischen Rat in Rom*, 22 November 1990, available at http://www.helmutkohl-kas.de
[2] Mikhail Gorbachev spoke of this pan-European dimension when, addressing the European Parliament in Strasbourg on 6 July 1989, he called for a CSCE summit to be held by the end of 1990, a call he renewed following the unexpected opening of the Berlin Wall.

for? How did it reflect the East-West convergence movement characteristic of what President Mitterrand called, in keeping with de Gaullian doctrine, the "end of Yalta"?[3]

The Charter was primarily the culmination of a dual-track process. First, it recognized the accomplishment of the stated objectives of the Helsinki Final Act of 1975. Second, it was driven by the changes in Soviet foreign policy that started in 1986: Mikhail Gorbachev's New Thinking gave tremendous impetus to the CSCE, whose follow-up meetings in Vienna from 1986 to 1989 laid the foundations for the document adopted in November 1990.

Nevertheless, the changes to the CSCE decided on in Paris did not go far enough to enable it to deliver a security and cooperation framework equal to the challenges that subsequently faced its zone of intervention stretching from Vancouver to Vladivostok. In the history of the CSCE, then, the Charter of Paris can be seen simultaneously as an outcome, an extension and a step.

- **1. The culmination of the Helsinki Process**

The Charter of Paris was first and foremost the outcome of a process that had started 18 years earlier and had produced its first benchmark document in 1975 in the shape of the Helsinki Final Act. The initiative in both cases came from Moscow. In the 1950s and 1960s, with the Central and Eastern European buffer zone proving not quite as docile as expected and the dispute with China threatening to destabilize the Soviet Far East, Khrushchev and then Brezhnev spearheaded a tremendous diplomatic offensive designed to talk the Western Europeans into a meeting of a European security conference at which they would recognize the political and territorial status quo in Europe, and especially in Germany.[4] The idea was also to work on uncoupling Western Europe from the United States by promoting pan-Europeanism.

In July and November 1989, when Gorbachev suggested holding a CSCE summit, the Eastern European satellite States were already slipping from his grasp: the Brezhnev Doctrine of Limited Sovereignty was repudiated by Gorbachev himself; free elections took place in Poland in June; the border between Hungary and Austria was opened in September; and regimes fell like dominoes in the aftermath of the fall of the Berlin Wall. Yet Gorbachev, like his predecessors, considered the "German

---

[3] Press conference given by the President of the French Republic following the Conference on Security and Co-operation in Europe (Paris, 21 November 1990), *La politique étrangère de la France. Textes et documents. Novembre-Décembre 1990*. Paris, Ministère des Affaires étrangères-Service d'Information et de Presse, pp. 53-56.

[4] Nicolas Badalassi, *En finir avec la guerre froide. La France, l'Europe et le processus d'Helsinki, 1965-1975*, Rennes, Presses Universitaires de Rennes, 2014.

question" to be the major concern of East-West relations and had no intention of letting the future of Germany out of his hands as easily as that. So even in late 1989, the Kremlin saw the CSCE as an instrument to serve the USSR's German policy. The Kremlin hoped to hold back the prospect of reunification by making the question a multilateral concern. At the same time, it had designs on turning the CSCE into a real pan-European security body that would strengthen the Soviet Union's foothold in Europe and prevent the humiliation of NATO expansion.[5]

However, in 1990 as in the 1970s, things did not go as planned for Moscow and it found itself compelled to review its objectives in the face of the Western camp's demands. Far from preventing German reunification, the CSCE was defined from the outset as a tool designed to help overcome the division of the continent. The countries of Europe and North America all agreed to the principle of a conference on European security in the wake of the Prague Spring crackdown, which convinced even the most recalcitrant – France and the United States – that it was best to take advantage of the keen Soviet desire for status quo to reshape the project, so as not to merely enshrine the Iron Curtain. As young people, students and minorities rose up across the Western world, many were those who felt that détente should be put to work for the people.[6]

So when the Western European countries embarked upon preparatory negotiations for the Helsinki Process in 1972 (the United States held back until 1974), it was with the intention of getting the USSR to accept a number of measures designed to improve all manner of East-West exchanges and weaken the Brezhnev Doctrine. The main thing, as French President Georges Pompidou saw it, was to foster convergence between the capitalist and socialist systems in order to gradually reunify the continent by rising above ideological differences. To his mind, the power of the "freedom bug" was such that convergence would inevitably be to the West's advantage.[7]

The CSCE's agenda was consequently divided into three "baskets" containing the different negotiating subjects. The first basket comprised a list of confidence-building measures designed to prevent any misunderstandings when conducting manoeuvres and military exercises along with the ten principles (the "Decalogue") supposed to guide relations between States. Among these principles were respect for human rights, refraining from the threat or use of force, non-intervention in internal affairs, and inviolability of frontiers. None of these principles established

---

[5] Marie-Pierre Rey, "'Europe is our Common Home': A Study of Gorbachev's Diplomatic Concept", *Cold War History*, 4, 2, January 2004, pp. 63-65.

[6] Nicolas Badalassi, Sarah B. Snyder (Ed.), *The CSCE and the End of the Cold War. Diplomacy, Societies and Human Rights, 1972-1975*, New York, Berghahn Books, 2019.

[7] Interview between Georges Pompidou and Edward Heath, 19 March 1972, Chequers Court. Archives Nationales de France, 5 AG 2 108, Great Britain.

Europe's borders, as the Soviets would have had it. Far from it, since the paragraph on the inviolability of frontiers came with a sentence regarding their peaceful change. Better still, the West managed to include in the Final Act the idea all ten principles were of equal significance: this meant that the Communist leaders had to acknowledge that respect for human rights was as important as state sovereignty. The second basket covered a vast range of provisions on economic, technological and industrial cooperation. And the third operationalized the "humanist" principles of the first basket with measures on the movement of persons, ideas and information. One track was dedicated to security and cooperation in the Mediterranean.

All things considered, although the Final Act could not be said to be liberal and was still far from a *Magna Carta* of freedom", it did run counter to the socialist regimes' prevailing precepts and practices. It took two years of intense negotiations for the Kremlin to finally accept these proposals after many concessions by the Western parties and in an atmosphere that was not always cordial: despite détente, the Cold War continued and the Helsinki Process was a product of it. Yet Brezhnev, who had made the CSCE a matter of personal importance, was anxious that the conference should not fail. The main thing was to obtain the principle of inviolability – synonymous in Russian with intangibility. The KGB would deal with the rest. However, as the history books clearly show, the creature quickly escaped its creator. Right from 1975, "Helsinki Committees" sprang up across the USSR and throughout the Eastern Bloc pressing for compliance with the Final Act.[8]

Although repression was swift, the CSCE had created a new climate in international relations in Europe. In the years that followed the Helsinki Summit, the regular follow-up meetings (Belgrade, Madrid and Vienna) and meetings of experts focusing on specific aspects of the Final Act – peaceful settlement of disputes, economic cooperation, cultural exchanges, etc. – monitored compliance with the measures and added others, with varying extents of success. The CSCE became a virtually permanent forum for all subjects relating to the Cold War, from the movement of persons to security to trade. Even in the most critical moments of the late 1970s and early 1980s, when tensions resurged over the Euromissile Crisis, the Red Army's intervention in Afghanistan and the Polish crisis, the two camps continued to talk. Negotiations never broke down and, to quote leading CSCE expert Victor-Yves Ghebali, the CSCE "de-dramatized East-West relations", assisting in such areas as the settlement of humanitarian issues.[9] Its multilateralism transcended the bloc-to-bloc mentality and the Soviet-American tête-à-tête, enabling neutral and non-aligned countries to participate in the discussions on security and cooperation in

---

[8] Sarah B. Snyder, *Human Rights Activism and the End of the Cold War. A Transnational History of the Helsinki Network*, Cambridge, Cambridge University Press, 2011.

[9] Victor-Yves Ghebali, "The CSCE in the post-Cold War Europe", *NATO Review*, 39/1, April 1991.

Europe. These discussions, with their press coverage whenever summit and ministerial meetings were held, showed the uniting force of the CSCE despite the ideological divisions.

The Charter of Paris took the Final Act to its logical conclusion. The end of competition between the blocs and the wind of freedom blowing through the revolutions of 1989 gave the delegations attending the Preparatory Committee in Vienna in July 1990 shared values and a stated will to engage in real cooperation, free of the vestiges of the Cold War. This volition took firm hold as events gathered pace in the summer and autumn of 1990: following the 2+4 Talks, the treaty that officially put an end to the Second World War was signed in Moscow on 12 September; and Germany regained its unity on 3 October. "Now," said François Mitterrand, "everyone is speaking the same language."[10] This time, the document adopted in Paris was clearly liberal, in the political sense of the word, as can be seen from the first part of the Charter, which acknowledged the end of ideological quarrels and took up the principles of the Final Act, now recognized by all: the primacy of human rights, the rule of law, economic liberty, friendly relations among participating states, and a common commitment to improved security. The second part gave "guidelines for the future": to build up the human dimension of the CSCE as well as economic and environmental cooperation; and take forward negotiations on disarmament and military issues.

On this last point, the Charter of Paris marked an advance compared with the CSCE's former role in this area. The confidence- and security-building measures (CSBM) adopted in Vienna in 1990 – following negotiations independent of the Preparatory Committee talks – strengthened the CSCE's military dimension. The measures provided in particular for a mechanism for consultation and cooperation in the event of any report of unusual military activity, as well as regular exchanges of information and visits to bases, all managed by a Conflict Prevention Centre.

• 2. *Building on Gorbachev's New Thinking*

The outcome of the 1990 CSCE was not what Gorbachev had in mind in November 1989 when he proposed holding a summit by the end of the following year. By the summit itself, George Bush and Helmut Kohl had cut short the Soviet president's pan-European dream: already, back in December 1989, the German Chancellor was siding with the American opinion that NATO should be the pillar

---

[10] Memorandum from the Directorate for Europe, CSCE, No. 305/CS, 28 November 1990. Doc. Vol. 82, 457-503.

of European security after the Cold War;[11] and Bonn and Washington agreed that a reunified Germany would be part of the organization.

Even so, the Charter of Paris owed a great deal to the Soviet leader. The remarkable convergence of views characteristic of the Preparatory Committee discussions was built on the New Thinking developed by Gorbachev in his speech to the 27th Congress of the Communist Party of the Soviet Union (CPSU) in February 1986 and in his book *Perestroika* in 1987.[12] This New Thinking was based on the observation that the confrontational policy of his predecessors since the second half of the 1970s had failed. Worse still, by stoking the arms race, it had ruined the Soviet Union and united the Western camp. A real détente was therefore needed, as much to prevent a resumption of Western hardening as to take advantage of Western loans and technology. Despite maintaining a stern view of the "imperialists", the head of the Kremlin nonetheless considered that the atomic bomb had changed the course of the world: common interests existed that extended beyond the class struggle, starting with the survival of humanity threatened with annihilation by weapons of mass destruction. War could no longer be seen as a way of destroying capitalism and promoting world revolution. This was a major break with Marxism-Leninism, for which many Soviet Union Communist party cadres would never forgive Gorbachev. Yet Gorbachev did not see it as challenging the underlying goal of socialism: to save "common human values". In this respect, the USSR needed to make an active contribution to international cooperation in the areas of human rights and cultural cooperation. The Secretary General of the CPSU hence felt that by leveraging themes dear to the countries of the European Community, the new face of Soviet foreign policy could expedite the process of East-West convergence and further the decoupling of the Euro-American duo. In actual fact, then, the traditional aims of Soviet diplomacy had not been forgotten.

And so it was in 1986 that the CSCE became the main stage for action on the Kremlin's policy shifts.[13] It is impossible to grasp the significance of the Charter of Paris without considering the decisive third CSCE follow-up meeting held in the

---

[11] On 12 December 1989, in his speech "A New Europe, a New Atlanticism" in West Berlin, US Secretary of State James Baker affirmed the primacy of NATO in the new European security structure, and consequently the *leadership* of the United States. The EC and the CSCE ranked behind, with Washington gradually restricting the CSCE to just its human dimension. Philip Zelikow and Condoleezza Rice, *Germany Unified and Europe Transformed: A Study in Statecraft*, Cambridge, Cambridge University Press, 1995, pp. 142-144.

[12] Mikhail Gorbachev, *Perestroika*, Harpercollins, 1987.

[13] In 1986, Gorbachev set a resolute course to apply most of the Final Act's "humanitarian" provisions in the USSR. For example, he had the law on the conditions for entry into and exit from the USSR amended in January 1987. He released many political prisoners and accepted the return of those in exile. He had the text of the Universal Declaration of Human Rights published in the press forty years after its adoption by the UN. And the jamming of foreign radio stations was abolished in 1988.

Austrian capital from 1986 to 1989, at which the sea change in Soviet policy was plain to see. Whereas, prior to Gorbachev, Moscow had always put security before humanitarian issues, essentially on the grounds of pacifism, the Soviet Union's initiatives in Vienna clearly marked the primacy of human rights over security issues. The Western states were so astounded that their initial reaction was scepticism of the Kremlin's real intentions. On the very first day of the meeting, for example, Soviet Foreign Minister Eduard Shevardnadze proposed that a meeting of participating States on humanitarian issues be held in Moscow to the consternation of the Western delegations, who initially saw the proposal as a trap designed to obscure the Soviet Union's real policy on human rights.[14] French diplomat Jacques Andréani reported a colleague's remark that, "Holding a meeting in Moscow on human rights is tantamount to celebrating a first communion in a brothel ..."[15] Despite the sarcastic remarks, the Western delegations leapt at the Soviet authorities' proposal to see just how far they were prepared to take the movement of persons, circulation of information and cultural exchanges.

At the end of the day, not only did this phase of the CSCE decide to hold three meetings focusing exclusively on the human dimension, but it also provided for the creation of a bilateral working group to address individual humanitarian cases and a procedure for cases where a signatory State sought to draw attention to a situation in another country. In addition, an entire series of specific commitments were made in support of family reunification and family meetings, and NGOs were authorized to attend CSCE meetings.[16]

This qualitative leap in humanitarian developments accompanied the considerable effort made in security: in addition to the conference on the confidence- and security-building measures, talks got underway between NATO and Warsaw Pact countries on reducing conventional forces and weapons in Europe. Here again, Gorbachev smoothed the way on 7 December 1988 with an announcement of the withdrawal of 50,000 Soviet troops from Czechoslovakia, Hungary and the GDR and the reduction of Red Army troops. The resulting Treaty on Conventional Armed Forces in Europe (CFE Treaty) was signed in Paris in November 1990, at the same time as the Charter.

---

[14] Telegram No. 30039 from Trémeau, 2 December 1986. Archives du Ministère Français des Affaires Étrangères (AMAE), Europe 1986-1990, Austria, Vol. 6165.

[15] Jacques Andréani, *Le Piège. Helsinki et la Chute du Communisme*, Paris, Odile Jacob, 2005, pp. 169-170.

[16] Andrei Zagorski, "*The Clash between Moscow and the Human Dimension of the CSCE: From Vienna to Copenhagen (1989-1990)*", in Institute for Peace Research and Security Policy at the University of Hamburg/IFSH (ed.), *OSCE Yearbook 2005: Yearbook on the Organization for Security and Cooperation in Europe*, Baden-Baden, Nomos, 2006, pp. 47-60.

The Vienna CSCE was consequently a major milestone on the road to the end of the Cold War, enabling the Western countries to gauge the full extent of the changes announced by the new team in power in Moscow. Nevertheless, the leaders of Romania, Bulgaria and the GDR remained highly averse to the human rights and religious freedom provisions. They sought all number of escape clauses, against the will of the USSR, which was more inclined to adopt the Western positions.[17] So not everyone was as yet on the same page when the third follow-up meeting closed in January 1989. But Vienna paved the way for Paris. With the opening of the Berlin Wall and the disintegration of the Socialist Bloc gathering pace, it became clear that the Final Act needed to be rounded out by a new benchmark document to gear the CSCE to the new situation. This adaptation work, commended by all the Heads of State and Government in attendance in November 1990, made the Paris Summit an important political step in the construction of the European post-Cold War architecture. However, it was not enough to turn the CSCE into a leading security player in Europe after 1990.

• 3. A step towards the institutionalization of the CSCE

The Charter of Paris effectively set the stage for the institutionalization of the CSCE. Its third part provided for political consultations between CSCE member countries to be scaled up with regular meetings of Heads of State and Government and the creation of a Council of Foreign Ministers. Alongside the Conflict Prevention Centre based in Vienna, a secretariat was set up in Prague and an Office for Free Elections opened in Warsaw. Despite these advances, the CSCE's international legal footing remained rudimentary in 1990: it remained first and foremost a political cooperation instrument, as it had always been. The Council of Ministers did not sit permanently; the Prague Secretariat had no political power and depended entirely on the decisions of the Heads of State and Government; the Office for Free Elections had no more than an informative role; and the Conflict Prevention Centre dealt solely with managing the confidence- and security-building measures. Security, as practised by the CSCE, was comprehensive security based on the interdependence of its political, military, economic, cultural, humanitarian and environmental dimensions. Where Gorbachev would have liked to have made it a collective security instrument, the Americans, Germans and French made sure that did not happen.

The fact was that, whereas European integration was propelled forward with unprecedented speed under the auspices of the French-German duo, and would culminate in the creation of the Single Market and the European Union, the institutionalization of the CSCE, depending on the form it was to take, bore risks that neither

---

[17] Memorandum No. 180/EU, 29 June 1988. AMAE, Europe 1986-1990, Austria, Vol. 6164.

Paris nor Bonn wished to take. For example, there was the risk that Moscow might seek to turn it into a collective security body so that it could impose its own security views, weaken NATO and achieve its long-standing dream of strategically uncoupling Europe from the United States.[18] Western Europe would then have found itself at the mercy of a resurgence of the Russian threat. This would have seriously jeopardized the strategic European project, which was in full swing with the reactivation of the Western European Union (WEU), the strengthening of the European pillar of the North Atlantic Alliance and, later, the Common Foreign and Security Policy (CFSP) in 1992. Another major risk of European integration being weakened by the institutionalization of the CSCE came from the opposite direction with the presence of the United States and Canada: their involvement in the second Helsinki "basket" on economic, industrial and technological cooperation might seriously weaken the Single Market and make the goal of a "European Europe" in economic and trade terms impossible to achieve. In any event, in both cases, the European Community ran the risk of dilution.

However, not playing the CSCE card also had its risks. As Washington pushed for NATO and Moscow sought to prevent the old popular democracies attach themselves to the West, the European Community risked being hampered by the maintenance of the two alliances or, at least, by the "new Atlanticism" championed by the Americans. Hence Hubert Védrine's proposal that the CSCE Summit scheduled for 1990 provide the opportunity to adopt a charter for Europe and an ambitious programme addressing as much the issues of borders and disarmament as economic and cultural cooperation.[19] It would also provide an opportunity to have all the participants recognize the role of the EEC in Europe and create institutions gathering 35 member countries.

At the end of the day, although the institutionalization argument was brandished by Bush and Kohl, it was in a minimalist version intended to convince the Soviet leader to accept that a reunified Germany should be part of the North Atlantic Alliance. At the NATO Summit in London in July 1990, Bush was careful to include the overhaul of the CSCE in his general programme to redefine European security by emphasizing the importance of the CFE Treaty and the role of the CSCE in supporting democracy in Eastern Europe.[20] By simultaneously presenting the contributions of the two main facets of the CSCE – security and human rights – the American

---

[18] Frédéric Bozo, "The Failure of a Grand Design: Mitterrand's European Confederation, 1989-1991", *Contemporary History* 17/3, 2008, pp. 391-412.

[19] Memorandum from Hubert Védrine, 13 December 1989, private archives. Quoted by Frédéric Bozo, *Mitterrand, the End of the Cold War, and German Unification*, Oxford/New York, Berghahn Books, 2009, 450 p., translated by Susan Emanuel.

[20] Speech by George Bush to the NATO Summit in London on 5 July 1990. *Verbatim record* C-VR(90)36 Part I, NATO Archives: https://www.nato.int/nato_static_fl2014/assets/pdf/pdf_archives/20141218_C-VR-90-36-PART1.PDF

president captured the very essence of the conference as an intergovernmental forum that had built its identity since the 1970s on the premise that democracy and respect for human rights and fundamental freedoms were essential criteria to ensure the security of individuals. In this way, Bush legitimated his vision of task-sharing between the CSCE embodying the humanitarian dimension of security and NATO taking charge of its military and political aspects. In this model, the confidence- and security-building measures remained dependent on the disarmament talks, over which the CSCE had no control. The Charter of Paris hence established the fact that it was not slated to replace the North Atlantic Alliance.

This state of affairs prevailed through the 1990s. Granted, the transformation of the CSCE into an organization was completed with the creation of a permanent council and a parliamentary assembly. The return of ethnic and sectarian wars in Eurasia led to the creation of a High Commission on National Minorities in 1993. The CSCE became the OSCE at the Budapest Summit in December 1994, with its headquarters in Vienna and with a Secretary General and an annually rotating Chairman-in-Office. 1997 saw the creation of a Representative on Freedom of the Media to "promote full compliance with OSCE principles and commitments regarding freedom of expression and free media"[21] in all the organization's participating States.

Nevertheless, the CSCE/OSCE still did not have the resources and prerogatives it needed to be able to safeguard the security of Europe and the former Soviet territories. It was unable to prevent the conflicts in the former Yugoslavia. It remained a political organization subject to the goodwill of its member countries and had no military means of coercion. In addition, the expansion of the EU and NATO's geographical coverage and missions gradually encroached on its fields of intervention and activities, even though this did not prevent it from cooperating with them. Most importantly, since the beginning of the new century, the OSCE's credibility has been undermined by Russia's incessant criticism as it seeks to preserve its influence in Eurasia, seeing the organization such as it is today merely as a restrictive and institutionalized vestige of the Helsinki "third basket".

So the days when the principles of the Charter of Paris were universally shared now seem long gone, especially with the end of the post-Cold War order and the many and varied challenges to the liberal democracy model, which have reduced the document signed in November 1990 to an emblem of bygone idealism.

Does this mean that, in the (short) history of the CSCE, the Charter of Paris stands as a failure? Would Russia have felt less humiliated and more of a part of the picture if the 1990 Paris Summit had gone further with the definition of a real new order for security and cooperation in Europe, as Gorbachev wanted? Might a crisis,

---

[21] OSCE Permanent Council, 5 November 1997.

such as that besetting Ukraine since 2013, then have been able to be averted? These questions are the subject of a heated debate in the community of CSCE historians and political scientists today, and we will refrain from answering them here.[22] But it does at least prove one thing: the Charter of Paris remains a benchmark document in the history of contemporary Europe and still embodies an aspirational ideal today.

---

[22] Christian Nünlist, Juhana Aunesluoma, Benno Zogg (Ed.), "*The Road to the Charter of Paris. Historical Narratives and Lessons for the OSCE Today*", OSCE Network of Think Tanks and Academic Institutions, Vienna, 2017, https://www.fesvienna.org/fileadmin/user_upload/documents/The_Road_to_the_Charter_of_Paris.pdf

TESTIMONIALS

French delegation at the Meeting of Foreign Ministers of CSCE Participating States in New York, October 1990.

In the front: Pierre Morel, Daniel Bernard (standing), Bertrand Dufourcq, Roland Dumas, Jean Musitelli, Éric Danon (standing), Jacques Andréani (back); in the back: Jacques Blot, Bernard Kessedjian.

Jean-Philippe DUMAS
THE ORAL ARCHIVES CAMPAIGN ABOUT THE CHARTER OF PARIS

To celebrate the 30th anniversary of the Charter of Paris for a New Europe, the Archives Directorate launched, with the support of Frédéric Bozo and Nicolas Badalassi, an oral archives campaign involving the main negotiators of the Charter of Paris.

The fundamental opposition between oral and written sources, which for a long time in France resulted in focusing on original archives, the sole medium for the writing of history, has gradually lessened giving way to a healthy complementarity between the different types of archives, which has greatly benefited research. Accordingly, starting in the 1980s, the Ministry for Europe and Foreign Affairs has conducted several hundred interviews with people working in diplomacy, political figures and ambassadors. The oral sources compiled greatly contribute to the accurate writing of historical events, reflecting the overall context and making it possible to take advantage of all the elements that go into making a political decision. Widely used by historians, this medium has contributed to the development of a new form of history and one that is not a mere memory of the past: oral archives answer new questions posed by political sciences, sociology and also the history of international relations. In giving various witnesses a chance to speak individually, they may even rectify failings of certain administrative archives, which present a situation in a succinct and supposedly objective manner, erasing the personalities and context from decisions.

For those who wish to study the end of the Cold War, oral sources are an essential supplement to paper sources. A period marked by extremely difficult East-West contacts was followed by multiple meetings, journeys and visits in which the main European leaders, Mikhail Gorbachev, Helmut Kohl, François Mitterrand and Margaret Thatcher, but also George Bush, decided to invent a new future for Europe. Late 1989 and early 1990 saw a huge acceleration of history: in a matter of months, entirely new issues emerged demanding unprecedented action from those involved, changing the way things were traditionally done in diplomacy. From a military point of view, it was crucial to build a new security architecture based on transparency and disarmament. But the political issues were no less important: the awakening of people liberated from the hold of the Soviets breathed new life into States, and with them national issues, borders, minorities, and, of course, displaced people and migration. The lifting of the Iron Curtain generated economic and cultural relations across the continent, suddenly giving coherence to a space that had long been separated.

Oral archives explain this complex process conducted at great speed. In France, to help end the Cold War, diplomats from the Foreign Ministry, and all the people working in diplomacy whether it be for the President, the Foreign Ministry or even the European Commission (Jacques Delors is mentioned), were called upon to intervene and put their relations to the service of the new policy.

Without claiming to be exhaustive, the campaign conducted by the Archives Directorate has sought to cover the various diplomatic networks as extensively as possible. The Elysée staff was interviewed, Hubert Védrine and Sophie-Caroline de Margerie, who, each with a specific role, shared their views on the President's action and reflections during this crucial year. In addition, contributions were made by Jean Musitelli and Pierre Morel, who, while having worked at other times for the Presidency, were working in 1990, the first at the Foreign Minister Roland Dumas' Office and the second on the Preparatory Committee in charge of drafting the Charter of Paris. Input was given by Marc Perrin de Brichambault, the future Secretary General of the OSCE, who was at the time, a diplomatic adviser to the Defence Minister Jean-Pierre Chevènement, and by Lucien Champenois, who represented France at the CSCE. The geographer Michel Foucher, often called upon during this period, agreed to share his views as a researcher and political adviser.

The excerpts published do not reflect all of the contributions. The interviews, which were not targeted, addressed a number of issues that were not of direct interest to the Charter of Paris and that researchers can discover by visiting the La Courneuve Archives Centre. Valentin Abeille and Marie Letamendia, students of Sciences Po Paris, were in charge of transcriptions and assisted by Madeleine Leroy, a student at ENS Ulm. This memory work was conducted alongside the work of Nicolas Dufourcq, the son of Bertrand Dufourcq, Head of the Political Affairs Directorate at that time.

Hubert VÉDRINE (1947)

After a degree in history, and study at the Paris Institute of Political Studies, Hubert Védrine chose the Ministry of Culture when he graduated from France's National School of Public Administration (ENA) in 1974 ("Simone Weil" year). In 1978, he took up a temporary posting at the Ministry of Foreign Affairs Directorate-General for cultural, scientific and technical relations.

In 1981, he was called to the Élysée by François Mitterrand, who appointed him as his Diplomatic Adviser, or "Technical Adviser on External Relations", until 1986. Upon appointment as *maître des requêtes* at the *Conseil d'État* in January 1986, he left the Élysée, only to return in February 1988 following the re-election of President Mitterrand, this time as Spokesperson for the French Presidency and Strategic Adviser. In 1991, he became Secretary-General of the Presidency. At the end of President Mitterrand's term in office, in 1995, he returned to the *Conseil d'État*. In 1997, he was selected by the Prime Minister, Lionel Jospin, and appointed Minister of Foreign Affairs by President Jacques Chirac. He held this position for five years. At the end of the cohabitation government in 2002, he established his own geopolitical strategy consultancy, in 2003, named "Hubert Védrine Conseil", while also teaching, travelling and writing. He is also President of the Institut François Mitterrand and an independent member of the Board at LVMH.

TESTIMONIALS

Oral Archives
Charter of Paris for a New Europe, 1990.
Interviewee: Hubert Védrine
Number: AO74_2
Length: 00:44:50

Interview dated 7 July 2020 with Nicolas Badalassi and Jean-Philippe Dumas.

How did President Mitterrand view the upheaval in Europe in the late 1980s?

From the very outset of his first term in office, Mitterrand was concerned with the future of Europe and the revitalization of its construction.

As early as 1981, during the Polish hunger demonstrations, he had said: "Anything that will get us out of Yalta is a good thing."[1] It was his vision of the future. Being the young know-it-all Adviser that I was, I passed him a note saying: "Mr President, if I may be so bold, there was no such carving-up of the world in Yalta. Stalin signed the Declaration of Liberated Europe – although it is true that he subsequently failed to apply it, but there was no cynical apportionment in Yalta. Those clichéd old criticisms, especially from Eastern Europe, are absolutely unfounded." His reply was: "Yes, yes, I know all that, but it's important for me to be understood." What this anecdote shows is that in 1981, already, he was thinking about what was to come next. Never mind the current commotions; his mind was already focused on what was to come afterwards, long before the demise of the USSR.

Indeed, later, around 1986-1987, when Helmut Kohl told him: "What's needed are some Franco-German initiatives in Eastern Europe, because everything is going to change", he replied: "Of course, but France doesn't have the same networks in those countries as Germany does; I'll go and pay them a visit first. Once those ties are revived, then we can take action together." Hence his tour of Eastern Europe, including East Berlin[2] but not Bucharest.

When crunch time came and everything started moving faster, in 1989-1990, Mitterrand felt that the upcoming phase should not come across as a resounding triumph, the domination of the West over a crushed and broken USSR. It was important not to humiliate the USSR, which meant thinking differently about the next chapter of relations with it. This was a man who had cogitated all his life over the 1919 Treaty of Versailles[3] and its consequences – and, conversely, over the victory

---

[1] Yalta Conference (1945): conference attended by the United States, the United Kingdom and the USSR aiming to outline the Allies' joint strategy for ending World War II and for the reorganization of Europe and the new world order.

[2] François Mitterrand's trip to the people's republics, culminating in his visit to East Berlin, in 1989.

[3] The Treaty of Versailles (1919) which reorganized Europe after the First World War.

of 1945. One had to consider all those countries becoming once again free and democratic, with their desire to join Europe.

Sensing that the European Union accession negotiations would be interminable, he floated the idea, very early, as early as 31 December 1989, of a "European Confederation". He was far ahead of the game, unlike those who accused him of having failed to grasp the situation. He put forward the idea, but it had not been adequately prepared. People in France and in Europe were not yet ready. Others were coping with emergencies. On the other hand, he was reasoning in a Gaullist, historic fashion, involving Russia, but not the United States. It was his most Gaullist moment, even down to the dissuasive tactics, but in this instance, it was all about the Europe of the future being able to orchestrate her own renewal. To him, it was crucial to include Russia, since Russia was on the same continent. Mitterrand never said: "It's time to break the Alliance with the United States." Obviously, the Confederation never entailed a renunciation of the Alliance, but it did embody a very European idea.

Obviously, the countries of Eastern Europe were openly hostile to the idea. For them, a connection with the United States was vital. The United States didn't even have to nudge them very hard. The project was nipped swiftly in the bud. Things might have turned out differently had the concept been presented in another way, perhaps somewhat later, after further preparation. We did subsequently try to give the project a second chance, at the conference in Prague,[4] in 1991, working with the one who was most hostile of all: Havel.[5] It didn't work, obviously. Havel only had eyes for NATO.

This initiative predated the Charter of Paris and illustrates that there had been multiple occasions at which Mitterrand had thought ahead to future relations among Europeans.

Baked into the idea of the Confederation was the desire to avoid humiliating these countries over the lengthy accession negotiations. He had said, back in 1989, that the negotiations would last fifteen years. The media were shocked: "But how terrible; he just doesn't get it! They need to join Europe right away!" And yet the process lasted... fifteen years. That was a point in time when France's political communication really did fail; a deliberate, hostile misreading by detractors, and a genuine misinterpretation from those who, despite their good faith, had not understood the manoeuvre.

---

[4] Prague Confederation Conference: assembly of 150 leading figures in Prague on 13 and 14 June 1991 to consider a new Europe.

[5] Vaclav Havel: writer, President of the Czech and Slovak Federative Republic (1989-1992) and subsequently President of the Czech Republic (1993-2003).

As Gorbachev's position weakened, as of 1986-1987, Mitterrand felt that it was important to organize the way forward with all partners on board, and thus avoid excluding the USSR, let alone the Russia of tomorrow. This was evidenced when Mitterrand, Kohl and Delors[6] invited Gorbachev to the end of the G7 in 1991.[7] Gorbachev went to London, but came away without the desired aid, owing to America's refusal, which sped up the putsch and its subsequent events.

In the autumn of 1990, after the trials and tribulations of the Confederation project, Mitterrand still felt that there was a need for all Europeans to come together under some kind of framework enabling realistic neighbourly relations with the USSR (at the time), as well as with the United States.

And the Charter of Paris, after the initial aborted attempt at a Confederation, launched prematurely into the ring, corresponded to this idea, like the single currency process.

In this, we can see a blend of the young Mitterrand's faith in multilateral systems and collective security – with the idea that, whenever possible, these are preferable to the unilateral use of force – and his convictions that had matured over his tenure as President. He tried in several domains; the facts remained unchanged, but there was a new context which made it possible to propose this Charter of Paris, in the autumn of 1990. It is consistent with his thought over the years. The new circumstances allowed for a more holistic, more specifically European approach. It all made sense.

How did the failure of the Confederation project go down at the Élysée?

With disappointment, to be sure. But we weren't naive – certainly not Mitterrand, but even the more junior, albeit experienced, among us. We had no idea what the USSR would become, nor Russia, but none of us were surprised to see that the United States didn't want any European self-assertion. Even the more open American Presidents such as Clinton or Obama, and the more experienced ones like Bush senior, who drew lessons from the past, were against anything that would attenuate American influence in Europe. So there was disappointment but not great annoyance; that's the way it goes. We had stuck to our roles.

---

[6] Jacques Delors: French politician, Minister of the Economy, Finance and Budget (1981-1984) and President of the European Commission (1985-1995).

[7] This was the G7 Summit of 1991 (15-17 July 1991), held in London and attended by representatives of Canada, France, Germany, Italy, Japan, the United Kingdom, the United States, the European Union, and Mikhail Gorbachev.

What was Mitterrand's position on the Helsinki process[8] and the CSCE?

Helsinki was a remarkable French initiative, thanks primarily to Jacques Andréani.[9] The idea of the third basket[10] was particularly shrewd. The Soviets were still sure of themselves at that stage, blinded by their confidence, and they agreed to the third basket. One can only wonder why. Internal pressure? In any case, it was extremely well played by the West.

But, to come back to 1990, Mitterrand was not particularly attached to any one institution over another. Everything depended on its usefulness at a given moment.

Mitterrand held that all available entities and institutions ought to be utilized. There was already a Franco-German framework, the wider framework of the European Union, as well as that of the single currency, and what was now required was a more global framework, Euro-Atlantic in the broader sense, but something other than the Alliance. It was time to feel around and explore which instrument would be the most suitable.

How did Mitterrand come to have such a special relationship with Gorbachev?

It developed very early on. Mitterrand had met him in March 1985, at Chernenko's funeral, and immediately noted: "He is completely unlike the others, he is different." Gorbachev was able to think fast and think for himself. At the time, the only other Western leader who thought highly of Gorbachev was, curiously, Mrs Thatcher: Gorbachev had visited Great Britain in relation to his agriculture portfolio. He held talks with Thatcher, who understood that this man was not just another spin-off churned out by a flagging Soviet system. While it is true that he was a product of the Soviet system, his impact was reminiscent of the John XXIII phenomenon[11] in the Church. Thatcher recognized this and Mitterrand, too, immediately. But other leaders were wary. Kohl said that it was a Leninist ruse, that Gorbachev was pretending to be different, but that he represented the same old Soviet system. Not unlike those who, even today, maintain that "the Russians will never change": it's the same way of thinking. As for Bush senior, he thought that even if Gorbachev were different, it would change nothing because there was the entire system to tackle. Mitterrand was thinking of the future.

---

[8] Conference on Security and Co-operation in Europe (CSCE): a forum for negotiation between the two Cold War blocs, active from 1973 until 1994. The Helsinki Final Act (1975) emanated from the CSCE.

[9] Jacques Andréani: French diplomat, Ambassador of France to the United States (1989-1995).

[10] Third basket: refers to the grouping of cooperation commitments regarding "Co-operation in Humanitarian and other Fields", which the Europeans imposed as a *quid pro quo* for assistance to the Eastern Bloc.

[11] Pope John XXIII (1958-1963), famous for his unexpected reformist initiatives when he called the Second Vatican Council.

Press Conference at the Paris Summit, November 1990.
From left to right: Daniel Bernard, Hubert Védrine, Jean Louis Bianco.

And relations between Mitterrand and Bush senior?

Exceptional. Admittedly, Clinton was more brilliant, Obama more charming, Reagan more charismatic. You cannot compare him to Roosevelt or Truman. But George Bush senior was remarkable for his knowledge of the outside world (so rare in an American) and for his background: he had been in Beijing; he had headed the CIA. He was a true professional. And his Secretary of State, Jim Baker, was tough but brilliant. Together with the President's Strategic Advisor, General Scowcroft, they were the best American team that I've seen yet.

Secondly, Bush is the man that Reagan had sent to Paris, since the latter was jittery about the Communists coming to power,[12] because, to his eyes, it was the USSR in Paris! He sent Bush, his Vice-President, to see Mitterrand. When Mitterrand met with him and explained his strategy, Bush was won over. He went back and told Reagan: "Mitterrand has convinced me. He's an exceptional man who knows the system inside out; we can work with him." Personally, that's how I remember Bush. Moreover, he always showed Mitterrand a kind of respect with

---

[12] An allusion to the appointment of Communist ministers in Pierre Mauroy's cabinet in 1981.

regard to his capacity for historical analysis, which turned into a friendship – and I don't mind saying it – which is altogether rare. Whenever Mitterrand spoke to Bush about French policy, which frequently differed from the American approach, for example regarding the Middle East, Bush would listen attentively because it was Mitterrand. He would understand because he was experienced and they would speak honestly and frankly about their disagreements and how to manage them. It was a true relationship. In fact, when Bush had to go, after the unexpected vote in favour of an outsider named Clinton, his last telegram was to Mitterrand. It read: "I'm leaving the White House in one hour. François, never forget that I am your friend."

Bush once invited Mitterrand to Kennebunkport, Maine, to the family's summer house by the sea. Only Dumas[13] and myself were there, with Mitterrand. We were dining with the Bush family when Barbara Bush said: "Mr President, we're going to church tomorrow, as we always do when we're staying here. Would you care to join us?" Mitterrand replied: "Thank you very much, I would be honoured, but there are some very important matters to which I must attend, some telephone calls to Paris. But Dumas and Védrine are here and I think that it would do them the world of good!" So we attended the church service – Presbyterian. Part-way through, the pastor announced: "We have the President here with us today and two foreign guests, whom we welcome!" And there was a round of applause from the faithful.

Since you worked closely with François Mitterrand, could you tell us how he developed his ideas on European matters?

It may sound trite, but it was the fruit of an entire lifetime's work. Mitterrand's first text reflecting on Germany and the future of Europe – the two are interconnected – is from when he was a prisoner in Thuringia: he was aged 20-22.

It means that throughout his whole life, he was turning these issues over and over in his head. Since he didn't speak English, people tended to underestimate his knowledge of international affairs. While at the helm of the French Socialist Party for ten years, he travelled everywhere; he met Kissinger.[14] These cogitations therefore stretched a long way back.

By 1990, Mitterrand had already been President since 1981. He could go back through old notes, conversations, anything that held value for him. The only useful contribution that advisers can make under a President like him is to add updated specifics, but they can never expect to substitute, with their short briefings, an entire

---

[13] Roland Dumas: French politician, Minister of Foreign Affairs (1984-1986 and 1988-1993).
[14] Henry Kissinger: United States National Security Advisor (1969-1975), Secretary of State of the United States (1973-1977). He is one of the pioneers of the *détente* policy (1963-1980), aiming to ease tensions with the USSR in the context of the Cold War.

lifetime of contemplation, of intellectual rumination. For European matters, moreover, he had some outstanding advisers: Élisabeth Guigou, Sophie-Caroline de Margerie, as well as Bianco, Attali, Musitelli, and others, and my own self.

Remember, too, that someone who is President speaks on a daily basis with other presidents, or high-ranking ministers. All of this gets taken on board and, after a year or two, one's understanding of the world is nourished by that as well. In the case of Mitterrand, there were conversations with Helmut Schmidt, then Helmut Kohl, and Jacques Delors, naturally. And so many others! Ultimately, he was as familiar with the issues as his advisers – with the exception of those who were with him throughout, at the very heart of the system. At any given time, the people with the most intimate knowledge of the global system are the leaders in office, their foreign ministers and just a handful in their entourage: three or four people, no more.

How did he envisage the end of the Cold War?

The foreseeable demise of the USSR would bring about the end of the Cold War. That could lead to a mammoth crisis, if not all-out war. Handling it was going to be an exercise in damage control, which meant maintaining very close ties with Gorbachev, supporting him while also pursuing a broader end-game, a European perspective, hence all of those proposals: the EBRD,[15] the brainchild of Jean Claude Trichet and Jacques Attali, was part of it; the Confederation if it had been successful; the Charter of Paris; the OSCE,[16] why not?

At the press conference following the Paris Summit, journalists quizzed the President chiefly on the Gulf War. It was almost as if the Charter of Paris, to their eyes, was a thing of the past.

A recurring problem, because the media these days focus on the present moment. Of course, it was certainly not a thing of the past: the Charter was an astute attempt to pave the way forward. The mere fact that journalists had finally grasped the imminent reality of reunification by no means indicated that every other issue had been settled! Indeed, even today there are clearly still deep-seated divergences across Europe's different regions. That could have been better handled politically and psychologically at the time. If the Confederation had gone ahead and the Charter of Paris had been better employed. All in all, the dissolution of the USSR was well managed. German reunification also. The break-up of Yugoslavia, very badly. As for subsequent relations with Russia, a complete mess.

---

[15] European Bank for Reconstruction and Development (EBRD): an international institution founded to facilitate the transition of the Central and Eastern European countries into the market economy.

[16] Organization for Security and Co-operation in Europe (OSCE): an organisation which took over from the CSCE in 1995, established as a forum for East-West dialogue during the Cold War on security and human rights. In turn, the OSCE, successor to the CSCE, espouses a comprehensive approach to security.

Jean MUSITELLI (1946)

A graduate of the *École Normale Supérieure* and holder of an *agrégation* teaching qualification in Italian, Jean Musitelli chose the Ministry of Foreign Affairs when he graduated from French National School of Public Administration (ENA) in 1979 ("Michel de l'Hospital" year). Assigned to the Europe Directorate, he was then posted to Rome in 1981. In 1984, he took up a position as Special Assistant on international affairs for the French Presidency, and subsequently Diplomatic Adviser, as of 1987. In 1989, he was promoted to *maître des requêtes* (and subsequently *conseiller d'État*, in 2001) at the *Conseil d'État*.

In 1990, he was appointed as Adviser to the Minister of Foreign Affairs, Roland Dumas, on the CSCE and later on the European Confederation. His duties included preparing the Paris Summit, in close cooperation with Pierre Morel, who represented France on the preparatory committee. After the Summit, he became Spokesperson for the French Presidency through to the end of François Mitterrand's second term in office. He then served briefly as Special Assistant to the Minister of Foreign Affairs, Hubert Védrine (1997), before his appointment as Ambassador and Permanent Delegate to UNESCO, where he remained until 2002.

Oral Archives
Charter of Paris for a New Europe, 1990.
Interviewee: Jean Musitelli
Number: AO108
Length: 01:34:53

Interview dated 30 June 2020, with Nicolas Badalassi and Jean-Philippe Dumas.

How did you come to be involved in preparing the Paris Summit of November 1990?

The decision came just after the CSCE meeting[1] held in Copenhagen[2], where the 35 members endorsed the idea of holding an extraordinary summit – since no ordinary session had been scheduled on the organization's calendar – in Paris.

As soon as the decision had been adopted, Roland Dumas[3] wrote, on 18 June, to François Mitterrand to inform him that our 34 partners had agreed to the proposed dates, from 19 to 21 November, and to suggest an arrangement in which, for the substantive preparations, he put forward "your former assistant, Jean Musitelli, to spearhead a task force for three months, and Pierre Morel to conduct negotiations in Vienna".

The President of the Republic accepted his Minister's proposal, and the preparations commenced in early July.

The very first thing that I did was to seek briefings from the leading officials as to the state of play with the project, and to see Pierre Morel in order to decide how our respective duties ought to be allotted, which turned out to be a very clear-cut matter. Pierre was to handle the negotiation side of things, right in the "cauldron" in Vienna, and my job was to arrange the overall environment and contacts with all of the appropriate administrations in Paris. The division of tasks came naturally.

In physical terms this meant that, over the preparatory committee's two sessions, while Pierre was based in Vienna, he would call me every evening: over and above his daily written report, we would discuss progress at length. He would give me his impressions, or describe the mood in Vienna, which he would not necessarily have conveyed in writing. For my part, I would brief him on developments in the thinking at the Presidency and at the Ministry, and logistics or organizational matters. And that was how we worked, with daily contact that kept each of us perfectly in the loop. If he had any declarations to make at his meetings, he would send

---

[1] Conference on Security and Co-operation in Europe (CSCE): a forum for negotiation between the two Cold War blocs, active from 1973 until 1994. The Helsinki Final Act (1975) emanated from the CSCE.

[2] Copenhagen Meeting: 5-29 June 1990, the representatives of the CSCE member States gathered in Copenhagen for the Conference on the Human Dimension of the CSCE.

[3] Roland Dumas: French politician, Minister of Foreign Affairs from 1984 to 1986 and from 1988 to 1993.

the drafts for prior approval. And on my side of things, I maintained close contact with the foreign embassies in Paris, especially those of the Americans, the British, the Germans and the Russians, so as to be able to exert the required pressure whenever negotiations hit a bump in Vienna.

At the time, there were two particular *chargés d'affaires* working at the Russian Embassy, named Krivonogov[4] and Orlov[5] – Alexandr Orlov was recently the Russian Ambassador in Paris – and we worked a lot with them under Hubert Védrine over the course of those years, since they were very pro-Gorbachev. Every single day, they would learn of further Gorbachev initiatives in real time, just as we would, and they were thrilled because they had the impression that their country had regained its capacity for well-thought-out, constructive action.

The third pillar of the arrangement was the executive secretariat, which was responsible for the actual physical organization of the summit. This was no mean feat, as it entailed building from scratch a suitable venue because Paris lacked an appropriate international convention centre. This is how the Kléber centre came to be expanded, with construction on the terrace spilling over onto the pavement of the Avenue Kléber, into a meeting hall able to host the 35 and their respective delegations as well as the observers. All of these aspects concerning the physical preparation of the buildings, the logistics, not to mention any sometimes thorny protocol issues, came under the remit of Pierre Dessaux,[6] who was in constant contact with us.

How was the Charter of Paris idea received overall?

The way in which this project emerged was unexpected; it was not on the diplomatic agenda. Gorbachev proposed it in Rome[7] in late November 1989. Mitterrand picked up the ball and ran with it. In answer to a journalist's question when he met with Gorbachev in Kyiv,[8] he simply stated: "Yes, if it could happen in 1990, that would be a good idea." A few days later, he suggested hosting the summit in Paris. It was a way of speeding things up at a time when, mere weeks after the fall of the Berlin Wall, Mitterrand was pondering how these recent dynamics could best be

---

[4] Oleg Krivonogov: Soviet diplomat, *chargé d'affaires* at the Soviet Embassy in France.

[5] Alexandre Orlov: Soviet diplomat, *chargé d'affaires* at the Soviet Embassy in France, then Minister-Counsellor at the Embassy of the Russian Federation in the French Republic from 1993 to 1998.

[6] Pierre Dessaux: French diplomat.

[7] 29 November – 1 December 1989: meeting between Mikhail Gorbachev and Pope Jean-Paul II. On 30 November, in a speech at the Capitol, Gorbachev returned to his "common European home" idea, advocating a progressive shift toward a reconciled Europe that could strike a balance between East and West. He mooted a new meeting, as of 1990, of the 35 members of the Conference for Security and Co-operation in Europe.

[8] Joint press conference by François Mitterrand and Mikhail Gorbachev in Kyiv, 6 December 1989. Full text available (in French) at: https://www.vie-publique.fr/discours/139603-conference-de-presse-conjointe-de-mm-francois-mitterrand-president-de

Roland Dumas and Jiří Dienstbier, Minister of Foreign Affairs of Czechoslovakia, in Prague, 9-10 June 1990.

French Minister of Foreign Affairs, Roland Dumas, visited Czechoslovakia on 9 June 1990 to commend the the first free elections in the country since 1945.

managed for the benefit of one and all. It was in that same spirit that he mooted his Confederation idea, one month later. This was also a way of affirming France's determination to remain present and active during the decisive phase now beginning, especially given the recent meeting between Bush and Gorbachev in Malta, two days prior to Kyiv, hinting at a reactivation of joint Soviet-American leadership. The Americans, for their part, saw how Gorbachev's position could be turned to their advantage, seeing their chance to apply pressure and thus accelerate the process of concluding the conventional forces agreement,[9] saying to Gorbachev: "Sure, no problem with a CSCE summit, as long as the agreement is signed before the summit." Baker[10] said as much in no uncertain terms to Dumas when he visited Paris in February 1990.

---

[9] In 1990, as the Cold War was ending, the Treaty on Conventional Armed Forces in Europe laid down new armament limits.

[10] James Baker: United States politician, Secretary of State of the United States from 1988 to 1992.

So throughout the final weeks of 1989, a whole diplomatic ballet was taking shape, one that would turn out astonishingly well. 1990 was to be a year of outstanding diplomatic and international accomplishments. The reunification of Germany was settled, the conventional forces issue was resolved and the Cold War was bid a solemn farewell. The Paris Summit stood, symbolically, as the culmination of this extraordinary sequence of events. All this resulted from a rather extraordinary planetary alignment: having at the helm a body of leaders with a sense of collective interest seldom witnessed in history, who built up a sort of collective understanding through unprecedentedly intense relations: more in-person meetings, myriad telephone conversations, discussions followed by correspondence illustrating the constant desire to compare information in real time: they were writing the script as they went along. There were no existing stage directions to follow. But the leaders who were writing it were careful to consider their partner's standpoint, seeking not to trip them up but rather to save the day for them – this was the case for Gorbachev – in the knowledge that this would lead to a more positive outcome overall. It was a clear affirmation of their shared, overwhelmingly positive will, which reached its zenith with the Paris Summit. Afterwards, things were to change dramatically. But that twelve-month sequence from the fall of the Berlin Wall through to the signing of the Charter of Paris was a masterpiece of diplomacy.

What was French diplomacy aiming for with its proposal to organize the Paris Summit?

The question in our minds was: given these complex circumstances, what can France do to ensure a continued role and a seat at the table, and more besides, in the process leading to the construction of the great Europe of tomorrow?

For Mitterrand, it was about who should be the architect of this great Europe. A race thus began between the breakdown of the Soviet imperium and the formation of the structures to underpin a reconciled and reunited Europe. The Americans, quite obviously, sought to pre-empt things, behaving as though they were the architects of the future Europe, with NATO as their trump card. And then there were the Germans, who, in order to obtain the best possible conditions for reunification, needed to find a *modus vivendi* with Gorbachev. And finally, there was Gorbachev, who thought that the future would more likely be decided in Washington or Bonn than in Paris.

So the risk that Mitterrand had discerned was that this Bonn-Moscow-Washington triangle would hold all the cards and that France would be relegated to a secondary role. I think that this explains why he felt the need, moreover, to come up with innovative proposals, above and beyond a mere recycling of institutions stemming from the Cold War and why, during his televised New Year's address to the nation on 31 December 1989, he solemnly proclaimed: "Europe is about to enter a new era. Previously dependent on the two superpowers, it will now return home

Roland Dumas' speech at the Meeting of Foreign Ministers of CSCE Participating States in New York, October 1990.

to its history and geography." This was the announcement of the Confederation. What it meant was: "France stands ready; it is taking up its place at the forefront of the process that is about to unfold." During the summit preparations, it was clear that the Americans wanted to keep control. In particular, they tried hard to make the ministerial meeting in New York on 1-2 October look like a key moment in the preparation and pre-empted the substance of the Paris Summit in an attempt to reduce it to a mere rubber-stamping assembly.

The conference in New York is also presented as the turning point when the Americans, traditionally reluctant followers of the CSCE, finally agreed to approve it.

It is true that the Americans, who had never shown much enthusiasm for the CSCE process, realized what they could get out of it to gain the upper hand over the USSR and nudge Gorbachev into making concessions on German reunification and on conventional armed forces. Bush played his hand well, with a Gorbachev who was in difficulty back home and was trying to avoid the USSR being side-lined during the construction of this new Europe.

But the New York ministerial meeting turned out to be a jamboree that changed nothing. And afterwards the preparatory committee's work resumed in Vienna, focusing on the finalization of the document. This is where the committee ran into problems: the format for the declarations (signed by 23? or by 35?), the status and remit of the Conflict Prevention Centre, which some, notably the Germans, envisaged as a kind of European version of the security council, whereas we (along with the British) viewed this as premature and preferred to bolster its role as a lever for transparency, management and information regarding military movements, without as yet turning it into a politico-military dispute settlement mechanism, encompassing any issues that could lead to security problems.

How important was the Paris Summit in the events of 1990?

Decisively important. What is paradoxical is that, in some ways, the Paris Summit produced successful outcomes even before it took place. It was a powerfully symbolic moment, in which the "reconciling the past" facet greatly outweighed the "preparing the future" facet. Several crucial negotiations were under way in parallel, starting with the Two Plus Four talks on Germany's reunification and those in Vienna regarding conventional disarmament. The inclusion on the Paris Summit's diplomatic calendar considerably boosted the progress of these talks towards a successful outcome. For Gorbachev, institutional consolidation of the CSCE constituted a guarantee that the USSR would not be left out of the imminent reorganization of Europe, which would otherwise give primacy to the European Community or NATO. For the meeting in Paris to be a success, all of the other negotiations first needed to be successfully settled. This led the Soviets to back down on the stickingpoints that had stymied negotiations. This positive result meant that the Paris Summit could become the climactic moment in which the former adversaries resolved the legacy of forty years of Cold War once and for all.

How did the CSCE Paris Summit dovetail with the idea of the Confederation announced by President Mitterrand?

No sooner was the Paris Summit behind him, than Mitterrand initiated his Confederation project. He was developing his ideas throughout the year of 1990, in his political conversations, especially with Kohl in Latche as of January 1990.[11] He discussed it with all of his interlocutors, and in particular those from Central Europe. During his visit Prague, on 13 and 14 September, he and Vaclav Havel[12] agreed on the idea of organizing a conference about the future Confederation in the Czechoslovak capital.[13] In this way, while the Paris Summit remained the priority

---

[11] Latche: located in the municipality of Soustons, in the Landes, south-west France. François Mitterrand owned a house there, where he hosted Chancellor Helmut Kohl in January 1990.

[12] Vaclav Havel: writer, President of the Czech and Slovak Federative Republic (1989-1992) and then President of the Czech Republic (1993-2003).

[13] Prague Confederation Conference: assembly of 150 leading figures in Prague on 13 and 14 June 1991 to consider a new Europe.

objective for 1990, the Confederation project was always in the background. And we very much kept in mind the need to safeguard what would be the future mission of this Confederation when defining the scope of the CSCE's development. It was during the Franco-German summit in Munich,[14] held on 17 and 18 September 1990, that Jean-Louis Bianco told me: "The Confederation is still on the agenda; it's very important to the President – actually, he was thinking of putting you in charge of it." On 21 December, the President sent a letter to President Havel designating me as the person responsible for preparations on the French side of things.

For Mitterrand, there was absolutely no contradiction in simultaneously strengthening the CSCE and developing the Confederation. The former had a proven track record of long-term effectiveness on security, disarmament and human rights. The Paris Summit had given it a new lease on life and a mandate rendering it the crucial body for stability in Europe. Its trans-Atlantic nature undeniably helped. Mitterrand could see how useful it would be to retain a trans-Atlantic connection over and above that of NATO, but in which all European countries, including the ex-Soviet ones, could take up their rightful place.

But the Confederation also answered a different need and another emergency which the CSCE could not: that of not leaving Central and Eastern European countries, released from the Soviet yoke, in free-fall, with dilapidated economies and societies impatient to access a Western lifestyle. For Mitterrand, this problem of rekindling economic, social, cultural and human ties between the two long-separated Europes, and of re-ordering the continent's space, was not a trans-Atlantic issue and did not belong in the trans-Atlantic framework. It was going to require carefully-considered solutions which, he believed from that point on, were not going to be clear cut or easy.

This later became very clear, especially when the Germans were pushing strongly for the Central and Eastern European countries' rapid integration into the European Community. Mitterrand, while not exactly applying the brakes, felt rather that immediate entry for these ill-prepared countries, all lagging well behind the Community average, particularly economically, would have disastrous consequences for their own economies in no way equipped to withstand such stiff competition. The idea was thus to arrive at some form of transitional arrangement that would enable a gradual catching up, facilitated by the renewed connections between the two sides of Europe. The Confederation was to deliver on this objective. It was to be a tool to repair Europe's torn fabric, requiring initiatives for economic action, movement of people, the environment, humanitarian work... These were all areas in which the

---

[14] The 56th Franco-German consultations were held in Munich on 17 and 18 September 1990, between the President of the French Republic, François Mitterrand, and the Federal Chancellor of Germany, Helmut Kohl.

CSCE's post-Helsinki[15] involvement was, despite its theoretical competence therein, somewhat underwhelming, with the exception of human rights issues, for which dissidents in the East brandished the Helsinki principles like a blazon of their rebellion and their liberation. Mitterrand took due note of the speeches made by the representatives of these countries at the Paris Summit, who were essentially saying: "Overcoming the ideological divide is a wonderful thing, but let us beware lest a new divide appear between haves and have-nots." The upshot of this was that, between the European Community, the CSCE, and the Confederation still in limbo, Mitterrand felt that the drawing board was large enough for him to design a pan-European framework capable of truly taking into consideration all of the difficulties regarding social and economic gaps, and development disparities across the continent.

Some of our partners were worried about the creation of a new institution in an already crowded environment and about the border issues that it might create. But Mitterrand, although not given to complicated contrivances, set great store by the usefulness of institutions if they genuinely satisfied a real need.

He believed that there could be no balanced development of relations between governments and among democracies without a solid institutional network fit to address all of the problems arising at a given time. That is why I was always careful, when it came to defining the Confederation's main areas of activity, to avoid any overlap with those of other entities and to ensure that they corresponded to identifiable and unmet needs of the countries' people.

Over the course of 1990, were any issues, such as culture, the environment, etc., transferred from the CSCE to the Confederation?

It would not be accurate to talk of a deliberate transfer. It was clear, however, that some of those issues you mention had been left to lie fallow by the CSCE over the previous years. And the same is true for the preparatory committee's meetings. With very few exceptions, the 35 showed little initiative on these matters, and failed to float any new or original proposals beyond the scope of Helsinki.

The context was such that interests became polarised primarily over security matters rather than economic or cultural cooperation and, when all is said and done, this was a logical reflection of the domain in which the CSCE had historically proven most useful and relevant.

In 1990, the priority objective was to channel the incredible dynamics that had been triggered by the fall of the Berlin Wall and its countless knock-on effects. It was important to ensure that the reunification of Germany occurred smoothly – peacefully and democratically – in accordance with the two conditions set forth

---

[15] Helsinki Final Act (1975): document outlining Europeans' mutual commitments on security, human rights and intergovernmental cooperation.

by Mitterrand; that it be of benefit to Europe, and not the inverse; and that it bolster the *perestroika* and Gorbachev in the USSR.

Given this backdrop, the way was sufficiently clear to assign the above-mentioned domains to the Confederation without giving the impression that the CSCE was being stripped of its remit.

At the time of the Paris Summit, what was the atmosphere like?

What I recall about the atmosphere is its immense solemnity and palpable emotion. But certainly not euphoria, nor triumphalism; rather, there was an over-arching feeling of having to shoulder a heavy responsibility given the upcoming uncertainties once this page of history was turned. The most remarkable thing was to see, for the first time, yesterday's adversaries gathered around the great table; the Americans and the Soviets, embodied by the two leaders, Bush and Gorbachev, who had worked the hardest to renew trust and pacify relations, and the freedom fighters from the former people's republics, such as Havel and Mazowiecki[16] and others, speaking freely and on an equal footing with their former masters. Prime Minister Martens of Belgium summed up the overall spirit by noting that the Paris Summit constituted "the highest degree of political consensus in international affairs achieved in a very long while".

The participants were nonetheless equally clear as to the difficulties ahead and the risks at hand. This was especially true for those representing the new democracies. Thus Hungary's Antall wondered "how to avoid the rusty iron curtain being replaced by an economic barrier between rich and poor, and ideological antagonism by economic and social disparities"; Poland's Mazowiecki worded it thus: "Beware an economic Yalta";[17] Bulgaria's Zhelev maintained that "the resurgence of nationalisms and old rivalries could become the biggest danger"; Romania's Nstase insisted on the need to resolve "the issue of national minorities, and to guarantee their rights so as to avoid their making political demands and courting separatism". Gorbachev, for his part, warned against "excess optimism" and highlighted the "risks that separatism and nationalism could lead to a Balkanization and even a Lebanonization of entire regions".

The question of military alliances was also central to the discussions. How to avoid the asymmetry looming large in their respective fates, with the scheduled liquidation of the Warsaw Pact[18] on the one hand (Gorbachev insisted on referring to

---

[16] Tadeusz Mazowiecki: Polish writer and statesman, President of the Council of Ministers of Poland from 1989 to 1991.

[17] Yalta Conference (1945): conference attended by the United States, the United Kingdom and the USSR aiming to outline the Allies' joint strategy for ending World War II and for the reorganization of Europe and the new world order.

[18] Warsaw Pact: military, political and economic alliance between the countries of Eastern Europe and the USSR. Concluded on 14 May 1955, the Pact was dissolved in July 1991.

its "transformation"), and the continuation, even strengthening, of the Alliance[19] as a trans-Atlantic pillar, on the other? The new democracies insisted most strongly on the rapid dissolution of the Pact. Antall,[20] while acknowledging Gorbachev's efforts, expected "the complete dissolution of the Warsaw Pact by spring 1992 at the latest". Havel showed similar impatience: "The Warsaw Pact is an obsolete vestige of the past and an instrument of subordination; it must be terminated quickly."

Their message was unanimous: the CSCE is all very well, but for us, the real solution is our integration in the European Community.

To reiterate, everyone was pleased to see the back of the Cold War, but had understood that no paradise on earth scenario was going to simply slot into place out of the wreckage of the Cold War. Hence the need to find some institutional framework that would make it possible to address simultaneously and coherently all of these complex and interdependent matters.

Did the Charter of Paris make it possible to anticipate the problems that were to follow?

As I said, the participants were clear-sighted about the problems to come. They tried to ward them off as best they could by buttressing the CSCE institutionally, so as to give its future actions more muscle. Ever since it was established in Helsinki, the CSCE, with its sporadic meetings, had seemed more of a process with regular meetings than a proper institution with all the trappings. The Germans were in favour (and this was one of our main sticking points with them) of further institutionalization, by endowing it with a permanent secretariat, frequent and regular sittings, and even a Parliamentary Assembly, perhaps formed on the basis of the Council of Europe's Parliamentary Assembly... France, however, aware of the risks of creating an immense white elephant, like a UN in miniature, was advocating a more measured, prudent and progressive approach, one that would preserve the CSCE's flexibility and make it more adaptable.

We reached the compromise that is reflected in the Charter, with a light secretariat and a Conflict Prevention Centre that was initially restricted to handling military matters. During discussions about the Confederation that were held some months later in Weimar, Genscher[21] was openly hostile to the project, stating that for the Germans the institutional pillar of great Europe was the CSCE, and the CSCE

---

[19] Alliance: refers to the North Atlantic Treaty Organization (NATO). This is the organization implementing the politico-military alliance between the United States and Western Europe. Designed to ensure security against the Soviet bloc, it was founded in 1949 at the outset of the Cold War.

[20] József Antall: Hungarian statesman, Prime Minister of Hungary from 1990 to 1993.

[21] Hans-Dietrich Genscher: German politician, Vice Chancellor and Minister of Foreign Affairs of the FRG and subsequently of reunified Germany from 1982 to 1992, serving in four cabinets under Chancellor Kohl, of whom he was a coalition partner.

alone. He would not countenance any pan-European institution embracing both Europeans and the Soviet Union without the presence of the Americans and Canadians. It was for this very reason that Havel, at first enthusiastic about Mitterrand's project, displayed increasingly grave reservations. The sense of the Soviet threat was still all too present in Central Europeans' minds. It is important to remember that at the time there were still 350,000 Soviet soldiers stationed in the GDR; 50,000 in Czechoslovakia; 70,000 in Hungary, and so on. No matter how often we reiterated that the Confederation would never be mandated to address security issues, that the CSCE was the only entity with a remit for confidence- and security-building measures, and that it was up to NATO to ensure military balance, there was still too much deep distrust of Moscow, and this was exacerbated by the rapid decline in Gorbachev's power over the course of 1991.

What was the Soviets' position during the Charter negotiations?

For Gorbachev, this was an important, delicate gambit. It was his brain-child; he needed to deliver results. Confronted with an acceleration of history he could not control, he viewed the CSCE as a way for the USSR to safeguard its place and role in Europe and in European affairs. He had observed the European Community's power of attraction for Central and Eastern European countries and understood the risks of the USSR's ties being completely severed not only with its former glacis,[22] but also with its economic hinterland. The Soviets' position was therefore to insist on further development of the CSCE's institutional framework, and the institution of periodic consultations. Particular importance was placed on the Conflict Prevention Centre, destined to become the model for future security structures transcending the alliances and able "to extinguish the sparks of any possible conflict", to borrow Gorbachev's words.

They were also proponents of a declaration of non-aggression among the 23 members of NATO and the Pact, proposed by the Americans at the London NATO summit of 5-6 July. This was our only point of contention at the discussions held in Moscow on 25 and 26 August with Pierre Morel and Philippe Guelluy, led by Roland Dumas. We were proposing, in keeping with post-Cold War logic, that this declaration be extended to include the 35 members of the CSCE. But the Soviets preferred sticking with the twenty-three which, in their view, had the added value of perpetuating the Pact. As a compromise solution, two declarations were to be adopted: one by the 35 under the Charter of Paris, and the other by the 23, separately. Pierre Morel had seen in Vienna that the Soviet delegation had been somewhat accommodating and discreet and were giving him less of a hard time than the American negotiator.

---

[22] Glacis: the USSR's satellite States between NATO and the USSR.

How did you feel about the Confederation project falling through?

The project's lack of success needs to be put in the new international context of the time. While 1990 had been a year of spectacular diplomatic wins, yielding a bumper crop of accomplishments, 1991 turned out to be a year of disappointments. It got off to a tragic start when, in January 1991, the independence movement in Lithuania was brutally put down by Soviet troops. From the month of June conflict flared in Yugoslavia, confirming the fears expressed at the summit about the destabilizing effect of nationalism. As for Gorbachev, already weakened, he never recovered from the thwarted coup d'État that summer and vanished from the political scene at the end of the year.

The failure of the Confederation was the failure of a tremendous insight. The guiding principle was that nothing sustainable could be built upon the rubble of the old order; it was necessary to invent a radically new concept. Things had been changing so fast over those eighteen months that not everyone's mind was yet ready to plan for the future, not even to start imagining a vague outline. The term itself raised eyebrows, so much so that during his speech in Prague, Mitterrand went so far as to say: "If it's the term itself that is upsetting you, then let's find another!" But the reasons why it fell through are not so much related to the project itself as to the assorted gaggle of objections that it triggered. "It's a project that troubles people," Mitterrand would say.

First and foremost, it troubled the Americans, who clearly interpreted it as a crusade designed to exclude them from the very European architecture that they believed they ought to spearhead. American diplomacy bore down hard on our friends from Central Europe, and on Havel in particular, to show them the risk involved in agreeing to be part of the same institution as the Soviets, devoid of the protection afforded by the American umbrella. For those who had just come through half a century of Soviet domination, such arguments certainly got their attention.

The Germans, as I mentioned, favoured the CSCE for the exact same security reasons and dangled in front of the Central and Eastern European countries the idea that the real solution to their problems, the only way to catch up with the development of the rest of Western Europe, lay not in joining this oddity, the Confederation, but rather in rapid accession to the European Community. They later arrived at a more realistic view of things because, with the problems they encountered integrating the former GDR, they soon understood the kind of cost and difficulties inherent in such an undertaking. So the Germans did nothing to support Mitterrand's project. Kohl was careful not to openly oppose it; he left that to Genscher. The difference of opinion was expressed in no uncertain terms, as I mentioned, at the meeting of German and French Ambassadors in Eastern Europe held in Weimar a month before the Prague conference, on 16 and 17 May.

François Mitterrand and Vaclav Havel at the Prague Confederation Conference, June 1991.

> Open by François Mitterrand, the Prague Confederation Conference brought together in six round tables some 150 prominent figures in charge of making concrete proposals regarding the European confederation. They are held in the spirit of the Hague Congress of 1948, at which the European community project was drafted.

Those who demonstrated an unwavering interest throughout were, for obvious reasons, the Soviets. Gorbachev felt that the Confederation concept encapsulated the "common European home" idea that he had mooted in 1987-1988, at a juncture when the Soviet Union could still hope to retain a measure of influence over its former domain. This interpretation amused Mitterrand, who explained to Gorbachev that the two arrangements were not exactly analogous. When I went to Moscow to update Vice-Minister Kvitinski on the Prague meeting's progress, I was welcomed with open arms.

Despite these twists and turns, cooperation with my Czechoslovak counterparts, led by Sasha Vondra, who was President Havel's Diplomatic Adviser, went smoothly and the Confederation Conference was hosted in Prague on 13-14 June in first-rate conditions. For his project's big debut, Mitterrand had opted for the more flexible format of a forum of prominent figures instead of the strict confines of an intergovernmental conference. He took his inspiration from the Hague Congress of

1948,[23] whence emerged the European Community, which left a powerful impression on him and which had been attended by political and non-political figures from democratic Europe. Together with our Czech partners, we selected 150 personalities from all European countries (as well as American and Canadian "observers"), hailing from civil society (business leaders, intellectuals, former political figures, artists, etc.), who were invited in a personal capacity, independently of their respective governments, to join in the discussions freely and put forward specific proposals for action in the five areas composing the Confederation's scope of activities.

And it worked quite well. There was a real dynamism among the six round tables that we had established: energy, environment, transport and communication, movement of people, culture and general affairs. A report was issued on each of these topics, offering an analysis of the current situation and proposals for action selected for their ability to reduce the physical and intellectual divide inherited from the recent past. There was agreement in the room to establish a permanent secretariat, to be headquartered in Prague, staffed by personal representatives of interested heads of State and government.

This was mid-June. We know how things unfolded in the latter half of that year. The Twelve concentrated on the goal of strengthening their political and economic union ahead of their December deadline in Maastricht. The Confederation dropped off the radar. The visionary turn of the century project was left in limbo. It was only in hindsight that the finest minds understood, reflecting on the European Union's subsequent vagaries, just how damaging that missed opportunity had been to the task of building a great Europe based on sincerely shared values and interests.

---

[23] The Hague Congress (or Congress of Europe): held 7-11 May 1948, it is deemed one of the founding moments of European federalism. It called for the creation, notably, of a Supreme Court and a European Assembly elected by universal suffrage, and advocated convertibility of currencies. Seventeen countries were represented at the Congress.

Pierre MOREL (1944)

Having graduated in law and studied at the Paris Institute of Political Studies, Pierre Morel chose the Quai d'Orsay when he graduated from France's National School of Public Administration (ENA) in 1971 ("Thomas More" year).

A diplomat at the Europe Directorate (1971-1973), then at the Policy Planning Centre (1973-1976), and later at the French Embassy in Moscow (1976-1979), he was appointed Ambassador, representing France at the Conference on Disarmament in Geneva when he was called to lead the French delegation in the preparatory committee for the CSCE Paris Summit: it was he who led, on behalf of France, the negotiations leading to the signature of the Charter of Paris.

In 1992, he was again posted to Moscow, this time as Ambassador. He then served as Ambassador in Beijing as of 1996, and to the Holy See as of 1996.

In 2006, he was seconded to the European Commission as Special Representative of the European Union for Central Asia, and then for the crisis in Georgia from 2008 to 2011. In 2014, the Swiss Chair of the OSCE appointed him Co-ordinator of the Ukraine political dialogue group, and the following year, Co-ordinator of the Working Group on Political Affairs for the Minsk process.

Oral Archives
Charter of Paris for a New Europe, 1990.
Interviewee: Pierre Morel
Number: AO107
Length: 00:45:09

Interview dated 30 June 2020, with Nicolas Badalassi and Jean-Philippe Dumas.

How did France deal with the upheaval in Europe in the late 1980s?

When the Berlin Wall fell, France's first reflex was to try to preserve the process of European integration, which was about to enter a new phase.

The President of the French Republic thus proposed a framework that had everyone somewhat intrigued: a European Confederation.[1] He had a far-reaching vision from the outset, in response to a continent-wide movement, which was going to require a whole series of new architectural components.

Without wishing to sound too introspective, I would say that he did have in mind a fully mature plan for how this project could evolve: he was very sensitive to context and to opportunities, but always with extremely solid anchors. We know that what was making the exchanges between Mitterrand and Kohl difficult in November and December was the former's insistence on safeguarding the European project, along the lines of: "Yes to reunification, but not at the expense of the European project." That was the crux of the Strasbourg Summit of 8 December,[2] a vitally important understanding.

With this incipient concept of a Confederation, Mitterrand sketched out an overarching approach: it was important that this work encompass the entire European continent, and the idea of an East-West Summit emerged. France lost no time in launching the idea that Paris should be the setting in which to approve the new arrangement.

In January-February, things started speeding up, even though no-one was as yet really sure how the GDR was to be absorbed at the end of the year; but everyone understood that the momentum was building and it was going to happen fast. The real sticking point was borders: ever since the Helsinki Final Act in 1975, the rule had been that borders were not to be altered, which the Soviets had insisted upon

---

[1] European Confederation: project floated by President Mitterrand with a view to absorbing the post-Cold War upheavals in Europe. This project was based on the values promoted by the Western bloc: respect for political pluralism, protection of individual freedoms and the right to information. It was introduced by Mitterrand during his public address on 31 December 1989.

[2] Meeting of the European Council on 8 and 9 December 1989: dual agreement on the principle of German reunification and the GDR's integration into the EEC, and on the realization of economic and monetary union.

in order to stabilize their post-war gains; but the West had maintained the caveat of negotiated changes, which was obviously going to be of primary importance for Germany's future.

Unification also implied the definitive consolidation of Germany's borders, which was necessarily going to involve the Four,[3] in other words the powers appointed by the Potsdam Agreements[4] to exercise authority over Berlin and Germany as a whole. Very early on, and very firmly, Mitterrand told Kohl: "My dear Helmut, it is time to give that crucial signal on the Oder-Neisse line,[5] still unresolved, because Germany has millions of refugees from the East (Silesia and East Prussia) and it's a delicate political issue." The French were really insistent on this point. Meanwhile, the Poles came to Paris seeking support. And Kohl's reply was: "Yes, of course, but right now I have my own political forces to reckon with, and it is already very difficult…" Mitterrand kept up the pressure, and the matter was settled in June through a parallel vote in the Bundestag[6] and the newly-elected East-German Parliament once and for all. It is fair to say that this major breakthrough helped speed up negotiations.

How did you come to be involved in preparing the Paris Summit?

Throughout the first half of 1990 I was in Geneva, where I was negotiating the convention on the prohibition of chemical weapons.[7] On the French side of things, the idea of the summit in Paris was finally accepted. In early June, the Ministers of Foreign Affairs of the Thirty-Five[8] gathered together and confirmed this ambitious event. From that moment on, the preparatory committee[9] could be formed, in early July, and the summit date was set for 19-21 November.

---

[3] The Four refers to the four Allied powers in 1945 – France, the United States, the United Kingdom and the USSR – who divided the administration of defeated Germany (and of Austria) into four occupation zones in 1945.

[4] Potsdam Conference (1945): negotiation among the Allies to decide the fate of the vanquished belligerents after the Second World War.

[5] Oder-Neisse line: the 472 km frontier between Germany and Poland, established at the Potsdam Conference (1945) and recognized by the GDR but not by the FRG, which hoped to have it altered. Upon reunification, the latter finally recognized it as the border.

[6] Bundestag: Parliamentary assembly of the German Parliament.

[7] Chemical Weapons Convention (CWC): international treaty adopted in 1992 which prohibits the development, production, stockpiling and use of chemical weapons.

[8] The Thirty-Five refers to the 35 participating States of the CSCE.

[9] Preparatory committee meetings for the Paris Summit were held in Vienna: the committee held its first session from 10 to 27 July, and its second session from 4 September to 18 November. Pierre Morel was the head of the French delegation.

Ahead of that deadline, everything simply had to converge: the so-called "Two Plus Four" negotiations,[10] which would lead to the Moscow Treaty of 13 September;[11] then formal reunification on 3 October, with the rights and responsibilities of the Four gradually being phased out. The orchestration of all this was rather subtle; Bertrand Dufourcq gave a very good explanation of the complexities of this suspension of rights. In parallel, there was an acceleration in negotiations on the CFE agreement,[12] which had already been under way for some time in Vienna under Ambassador François Plaisant[13] and his team.

These were highly technical exercises, but all concerned realized that they were part of a broader framework, with a tight deadline and tremendously high stakes: for more than forty years, the "Cold War" had stood as a massive security infrastructure, with the confrontation of forces in the event of conflict, already prepared and battle-ready. Even though the political tension had eased, this gargantuan military system remained in place across the continent, stretching along the line separating East from West.

Our work was thus conducted under extreme pressure. I left my negotiations on chemical weapons in Geneva and was told: "You are to drop all of that, leave it to your deputy, and head to Vienna for some very intense sessions that will last through the summer and until mid-November."

During the initial improvization period, I must say that I was greatly assisted by a team of young, highly responsive, dynamic diplomats. We divided up our workload, sharing out the different sectors, and settled into a sustained pace of work in a room in the Hofburg[14] which, although not yet fully reconfigured, was the conference venue provided by Austria. While the 1975 Helsinki Final Act gave us a basis on which to work, the message was: "Don't pad it out with additional paragraphs. You are there to design a new chapter in Europe's security and cooperation."

We swiftly introduced the time-honoured mechanisms used in multilateral fora, holding prior consultations before the formal sittings opened. First we would hold a European meeting, and then there would also be a meeting of the member

---

[10] The "Two Plus Four" negotiations were held between representatives of the two German States and the Four Powers, to settle various foreign policy issues stemming from Germany's reunification in 1990.

[11] Treaty on the Final Settlement with Respect to Germany (1990): international agreement between the Two Plus Four countries, paving the way to German reunification.

[12] The Treaty on Conventional Forces in Europe (CFE) was signed in Paris on 19 November 1990 by 34 representatives of NATO and of the Warsaw Pact. The CFE Treaty limited the volume of weapons and conventional equipment that signatory States might deploy within its region of application, and provided for the destruction of tens of thousands of heavy weapons.

[13] François Plaisant: French diplomat, Ambassador representing France in the Vienna negotiations on conventional armed forces and on confidence- and security-building measures in Europe (1989-1991).

[14] The Hofburg: current residence of the Republic of Austria's Federal President.

countries of the Alliance. For us, it was vital to have our discussions among Europeans first, and only then meet with the Allies. Obviously, this preliminary private huddle used to irritate the Americans: a classic tactic, which began in Helsinki. I remember when it all began in 1973.

There were also consultations going on discreetly behind the scenes, like an unmentioned open secret, between the four Western powers: the United States, the United Kingdom, Germany and France. We used to have lunch together on an almost weekly basis and establish a step-by-step framework, trying to establish waypoints to guide our work. The Austrians, who ran the Secretariat, wanted to understand where to tread, and had, separately, set up rather an original system, which turned out to be quite useful, with the Soviets, the Germans, the British, and the French, to compare viewpoints in an Austrian manner, and thus bring the two sides closer together. I would tease them by saying: it's a gathering of the former empires!

Vienna is a most pleasant capital ; not too large, nor too complicated, and so it was easy to get around and hold consultations before meeting up at the Hofburg. Those famous Viennese cafés were the perfect places for our paths to cross, repeatedly. Everyone would glean as much information as possible ; all of this work had a sort of parliamentary feel to it, with thirty-five delegations all under pressure.

How would you assess the Charter of Paris now, in hindsight?

In terms of its substance, of course, we saw some dreadful repercussions quite early on but, when all is said and done, the framework held firm. The Charter remains the foundational text. No other standards have been established since then, even though the Europe that we thought we had glimpsed, with doubtless no small measure of optimism, did not take on the desired shape.

Obviously, there was a brutal call to order when the war in Yugoslavia broke out, although it could be argued that the Balkans have always been prone to considerable tensions and confrontations over very localized issues. But on the whole, these setbacks must be set against the achievement of having dismantled Europe's machine of self-destruction and division.

And since then, whenever things get out of hand anywhere, the OSCE is called in to help. Discreetly, over the decades, the OSCE has performed an incredible feat of safeguarding and stabilization, which might not steal the headlines but which is nonetheless indispensable. This is an organization that is widely under-estimated, but still very useful.

I care deeply about it, because I was there at the beginning: during preparations in 1973, there were fewer than a hundred of us in the Aalto University's Dipoli building, in the outskirts of Helsinki. In Vienna, everything had by then been enormously scaled up, since it had already become a very codified mechanism. But back in Helsinki, this was the first continent-wide gathering: you could just as easily run into a clergyman who was there to represent the Holy See as you could one of the "dinosaurs" from the Cold War era. Zorin[15] was a pure product of the Stalinist era, and there was also the representative of Salazar,[16] since this was before the Carnation Revolution of 1974.

How important was the CSCE and the Helsinki process to President Mitterrand?

Mitterrand was haunted by the risk of losing control over a process that could rouse the demons of war in Europe. I was in a position to witness this even more closely in subsequent years when I was Diplomatic Adviser. Whenever he met with his counterparts, he would slip the subject into the conversation: "it is crucial that we never let the situation slip through our fingers because with Europe's past, its fate, the risks are enormous". This involved ensuring that nothing was ever done without first factoring in the Soviets. Hence the difficult but constant dialogue with Moscow and the importance of the rules set forth in Helsinki. In this respect, he embodied, in his own way, a great deal of continuity from General de Gaulle, Pompidou and Giscard.

In this extraordinary CSCE summit in Paris, there was something for everyone. Of course, I am simplifying, but the Neutral States felt that they regained the role that they had played fifteen years prior, in Helsinki and in Geneva. Although the USSR may have been upset, the consolidation of the CSCE's framework was nonetheless seen as a stabilizing factor, a shield against the unknown. As for Germany's neighbours and the members of the Atlantic Alliance more broadly, the Two Plus Four negotiations had excluded them: in Vienna and subsequently in Paris, they were given a place at the table.

Take, for instance, the heavyweights themselves: there were advantages here for them, too. For Washington and London, keeping Germany in the Alliance was essential; the old Soviet dream of a neutral Germany was ruled out, by unanimous agreement.

For their part, the Germans achieved the peaceful consecration of their unity, and not merely as an arrangement among leading powers: each and every country subscribed to it. Germany regained its capital and ceased to be historically suspect, if you will: the German question was settled once and for all. This was an immense relief, a historic turning point.

---

[15] Valerian Alexandrovich Zorin: Soviet diplomat and politician, permanent representative of the USSR to the UN Security Council (1953-1953 and 1956-1965), Soviet Ambassador to the FRG (1955-1956) and to France (1965-1971).

[16] António de Oliveira Salazar: Portuguese economist and politician, President of Portugal's Council of Ministers (1932-1968).

For France, finally, this summit spelled the end of the "Europe of Yalta", mapped out without France's input in 1944. Relegating this to the history books had been a diplomatic and strategic ambition nurtured by every President of France's Fifth Republic: the Atlantic alliance was maintained, albeit with certain French complexities; the Warsaw Pact was to vanish; and European integration was to get a second wind. There were still large areas of uncertainty, of course, but France had participated fully in all of the negotiations that ultimately converged in Paris. Concluding the summit to close by hosting all of the heads of State and Government in Versailles might have appeared "over the top" at first glance, but it was only fitting that this historic occasion should be marked in an eminently symbolic location which, for more than a century, had witnessed the unfolding and the resolution of so many dramas.

Sophie-Caroline de MARGERIE (1956)

With degrees in public law and English literature, and having studied at the Paris Institute of Political Studies, Sophie-Caroline de Margerie chose the Ministry of Foreign Affairs when she graduated from France's National School of Public Administration (ENA) in 1980 ("Voltaire" year). She was appointed to the Directorate-General for cultural, scientific and technical relations and subsequently in the legal directorate, before being recruited by the *Conseil d'État* in 1986.

In June 1988, she joined the Élysée as Special Assistant on international and strategic affairs to the Diplomatic Adviser. In 1990, she monitored the negotiations on international aspects of Germany's reunification. In November, she took over from Elisabeth Guigou when the latter was appointed Minister Delegate for European Affairs, thus becoming President François Mitterrand's Technical Adviser on European Affairs. She assisted with the negotiations leading to the Maastricht Treaty.

In 1992, she was promoted to *maître des requêtes*, and subsequently *conseiller d'État*, in 2005, at the *Conseil d'État*.

Oral Archives
Charter of Paris for a New Europe, 1990.
Interviewee: Sophie-Caroline de Margerie
Number: AO109
Length: 55:03

Interview dated 7 July 2020, with Nicolas Badalassi and Jean-Philippe Dumas.

What was your experience, at the Élysée, of the upheavals in Europe of 1989?

President Mitterrand had decided to commence his second term of office with visits to Central and Eastern Europe. He went to Poland in June 1989, between the two rounds of the first free elections to be held in the country for a very long time. This trip was quite moving for me because my father is Polish. For those who made the journey, it was a first realization of the changes afoot in the East, starting in Poland.

In very early November 1989, a few months later, I was in Berlin – just before the Wall came down. I had not been sent by the Élysée; I was part of a working group at the Aspen Institute in Berlin. The group included diplomats, politicians, journalists, all young Europeans from both the East and the West. Once we arrived, on the Western side of course, someone offered us the chance to go over to East Berlin, saying: "Things are moving, there are people to meet, there are lots of movements emerging, lots of people coming together; would you be interested in going to see them?" Our answer was: "Of course." There was a young minister from the German government in our group, who called Bonn to get permission to cross over to the East; it was granted. We went through Checkpoint Charlie one evening, and found ourselves in an apartment with people from the *Neues Forum*[1] and other movements, and we all got talking. Those people were not discussing *Wiedervereinigung*, reunification, at all; rather, they were talking about restoring democracy, about transforming their country. Along with all the other members of my group, I felt sure that this country was fast approaching boiling point. Upon my return, I said as much at the Élysée. It was a privileged glimpse of the changes to come, although at the time we had no idea of their magnitude, nor their rapidity.

What subsequent role did President Mitterrand play in the process of Germany's reunification?

President Mitterrand had long been in direct and frequent contact with the Chancellor, as had the Élysée team with their counterparts in the Chancellery. Yet the Chancellor never forewarned him of his ten-point programme for achieving

---

[1] *Neues Forum*: a political movement in East Germany formed in the months prior to the fall of the Berlin Wall, with the aim of stimulating dialogue on democratic reforms, so as to reshape society.

Germany's reunification. The ten-point programme, that was 28 November. Before that, there had been a dinner in Paris, a European Council dinner. Jacques Delors[2] was there. As far as I recall, there was never any mention of reunification. It was the elephant in the room. Everyone was thinking about it, but no-one talked about it.

In any case, the overall impression at the Élysée was that Kohl was playing his cards quite close to his chest. Did he already know exactly what he wanted at that time? One thing that was certain – at least that was how we saw it – was that he had an agenda, and that he intended to push it through.

François Mitterrand's role, performed quite successfully, was to convey to him that this was naturally, and primarily, a German question, but that it was also a European question, and that it furthermore concerned other players, notably the Four Powers, which, ever since the Potsdam Agreement[3] had certain responsibilities regarding Berlin. Dialogue was thus not exactly *imposed*, but was nonetheless the subject of, shall we say, constant reminders made by the President to the Chancellor; Franco-German cooperation, certainly, and more broadly, the imperative of resolving everything in a European and international framework.

Very early in the piece, the President set forth the principles that he felt ought to guide not only these changes, but also reunification. At which precise juncture did it become apparent that we were heading inevitably, at a greater or lesser speed, toward reunification? I cannot say. But the President had stated at the outset: "It needs to be done peacefully, in a much wider framework, with agreement from the neighbours, agreement from the Powers, and democratically." For him, this meant ensuring that the peoples were consulted, that their will be registered and acted upon – he was thinking of the East German people – and furthermore that the change occur in tandem with a deepening of the European integration process. These principles, which came to him very early on, he enunciated them very early on, and ultimately, it more or less happened as he had envisioned it.

President Mitterrand's involvement in the reunification of Germany was criticized.

President Mitterrand visited the GDR in December 1989. The trip was indeed controversial in France. I think that there were several reasons for that. The trip was criticized because it was interpreted as proof of his intention to hinder the process leading to reunification. I believe that it was inspired, rather, by the President's intention to see for himself what was actually going on, to talk with students, to discuss matters, obviously, with officials, to see which changes people hoped would be made in the country.

---

[2] Jacques Delors: French statesman, President of the European Commission from 1985 to 1995.

[3] Potsdam Agreement: signed at the end of the Potsdam Conference, held from 17 July to 2 August 1945. It was the third meeting, following those of Tehran and Yalta, among the leading Allied powers (USSR, United States, United Kingdom, and France).

TESTIMONIALS

Press Conference with Helmut Kohl and François Mitterrand at the Élysée Palace at the 55th Franco-German Summit on 25-26 April 1990.

On the eve of the extraordinary European Council meeting in Dublin on 28 April 1990, Helmut Kohl and François Mitterrand officially announced their wish to move forward rapidly down the path towards the Economic and Monetary Union.

Just before the visit, I went to the GDR on a preparatory mission with the Head of Protocol, which is standard practice ahead of official trips. And I remember feeling increasingly surprised as the mission unfolded. We had arrived, as we always did, with a tentative programme for the President, and our job was to see whether or not, on a practical level, those plans were feasible, for example concerning travel times, and also, and above all, to identify his interlocutors and the issues to be discussed. And that was when it hit home; all the people with whom I spoke, who were obviously not the President's interlocutors, but rather, their staff, were saying: "Listen, we simply cannot commit right now, neither in terms of the substance of their talks, nor as to whether the meeting can actually go ahead at all, because it is possible that everything could change by the time the President gets here in two weeks." It was thus extremely difficult to set out a programme because the whole thing was peppered with questions marks.

When I got back to the Élysée, I prepared my mission report, and I concluded my brief to the President by saying that it would be better not to proceed with the trip, because the country was – even in the words of its officials – in total anarchy. The President telephoned me, something which he had never done before: "So, if I am to understand you correctly, you are advising me to cancel this trip." To which I had to reply: "Yes, Mr President." And it was hard to say that "Yes" because the trip had been on the President's schedule for a long time, and what I was saying bore tremendous responsibility, but that was my honest opinion. He said to me: "I'll think about it, I'll see."

And two days later I heard him saying, on the television: "In a few days I will be going to the GDR."

By taking that trip, the President was able to assess the situation, as was his intention, but he did perhaps miss an opportunity to say, when he was there, that he understood the desire for reunification, which, at that moment, was already perceptible – things had moved since early November – and also to show his solidarity with the Chancellor and with Germany. He didn't do it when he had the chance; there was no symbolic gesture like the hand-in-hand moment in Verdun, nothing that conveyed to the German public – I don't think that Chancellor Kohl himself harboured any doubts as to the President's solidarity – that France was supportive. Something was missing in my opinion.

President Mitterrand suggested a Confederation as a way of orienting developments in Europe.

On the subject of the Confederation, all I can say is that the President first mooted the idea in December 1989[4], the evening of his seasonal greetings. To the surprise of his staff.

Had you not been forewarned at all?

No. But then the President was not in the habit of announcing things to his staff, nor of debriefing them, for that matter. Unlike Michel Rocard,[5] he was not into brainstorming. Collective deliberations were not the modus operandi at the Élysée. Decisions were made, rather, after one-to-one discussions and exchanges of notes; it was a different way of working.

---

[4] On 31 December 1989, François Mitterrand expressed his wish to create a European Confederation that would encompass the entire continent, so as to help establish a new post-Cold War European order.

[5] Michel Rocard: French politician, Prime Minister from 1988 to 1991.

How much importance did he place on this project?

The Confederation Conference[6] took place in the summer of 1991. The President had set great store by it. He truly believed in this idea. To his mind, the Charter of Paris was indispensable, of course, since the CSCE was the logical forum in which to solemnly and officially lay the Cold War to rest. The Confederation, from the President's perspective, would offer the countries of Central and Eastern Europe a setting in which to rekindle their relations with those of the Community, in the expectation, a constructive expectation, of accession in the future.

Unfortunately – although it is hardly very surprising when you think of everything that these Central European countries had been through – the idea was not widely embraced by the intended beneficiaries, these self-same Central European countries, and Czechoslovakia in particular. Again, this was hardly surprising, because the notion of keeping the US out and bringing the Soviet Union in was precisely what they wanted to avoid. They wanted the American umbrella; they didn't want any more Soviet oversight.

To go about explaining, therefore, – as we did – that it made sense, geographically and politically, and that it was in no way a reconstituted Warsaw Pact,[7] simply did not go down well. What is more, the Americans were against it, and took action accordingly. But all the way through, the President wanted it, and firmly believed in it, and encouraged us to give it more thought, put our ideas in writing and talk with our interlocutors.

I remember being present at a particular luncheon with President Havel[8] at the Élysée Palace. I was seated next to the Czechoslovak Foreign Minister, Prince Karel Schwarzenberg[9]. It was a luncheon for twelve people, rather a small affair, and Havel was noticeably ill at ease. Anyone who observed his body language and heard his tone when he spoke could see that this project was being pushed on him: he was not in favour of it and could not lend his support.

---

[6] This conference was held in Prague, 13-14 June 1991, and brought together some 150 prominent personalities (from the politics, business, culture, etc.) whose work centred on six major areas: culture, movement of people, communications, energy, the environment and issues of a more general nature.

[7] Warsaw Pact: a former military alliance formed on 14 May 1955 among the majority of the Soviet Bloc communist countries, and which was dissolved in July 1991.

[8] Vaclav Havel: Czechoslovak playwright, essayist and statesman, President of the Czech and Slovak Federative Republic (1989-1992) and subsequently President of the Czech Republic (1993-2003).

[9] Karl Schwarzenberg: Czech politician, close advisor to President Vaclav Havel in the early 1990s.

What was President Mitterrand's involvement in the treaty settling the border issue between Germany and Poland?[10]

The President wanted Chancellor Kohl to reaffirm the Oder-Neisse line[11] and its intangible and inviolable nature; that the proclamation of this inviolability and intangibility appear in a bilateral agreement rather than be made unilaterally; and that this all occur as soon as possible. On the substance, the Chancellor had absolutely no objections, but he had qualms about the *tempo* – "I will get around to it" – and the immediately contractual nature that such recognition was to entail. For him, it was a delicate internal political matter, and he wanted to deal with it as best suited him. The President kept hounding him about it, saying: "It is very important for Poland that this issue be resolved, and it is important more broadly for Europe as a whole." This really was one of the quite sensitive topics between the two of them, on which the President greatly insisted, upon the request, obviously, of the Poles, who had seen him as an ally. But he wasn't doing it just to keep Poland happy; it was because he really did see it as an absolutely vital issue, and that the Polish demands were wholly legitimate in this regard. He was also focused on Germany's renunciation of nuclear weapons.

The notion of borders is central in the Charter of Paris. Was that at the behest of Poland?

Yes, there had been a Polish request. There had been a visit to Paris by General Jaruzelski[12] and by his Prime Minister Mazowiecki[13] with regard to this very subject.

To what extent were economic issues included in the proposals made by President Mitterrand in 1990?

There was an economic agenda, with the European Commission at the heart of the arrangement; the Confederation was envisaged as a kind of sluice – although the President did not actually use such a term – or a stepping stone toward something that would result in these countries' accession to the Community. The prospect of accession was definitely there.

---

10   The German-Polish Border Treaty: signed 14 November 1990, the treaty settled the border issue between Germany and Poland that had been pending since 1945.

11   Oder-Neisse line: the border between East Germany and western Poland, determined by the Allies at the end of the Second World War, and formed by two rivers: the Oder and the Neisse.

12   Wojciech Witold Jaruzelski: Polish statesman and military officer, President of the Republic of Poland from 1989 to 1990.

13   Tadeusz Mazowiecki: Polish writer and statesman, President of the Council of Ministers of Poland from 1989 to 1991.

How would you judge Chancellor Kohl's role, retrospectively?

Everybody acted truly responsibly. The framework within which all of these events were being addressed and settled was constructed in record time, and it held firm. Apart from President Mitterrand, if anyone else is particularly praiseworthy, it is the Chancellor, who understood the political opportunity before him, the historic importance of the event, and that he could not go it alone. He had to take political risks regarding the border, as well as on economic and monetary union. There were no foregone conclusions, and these leaders handled everything with a great sense of responsibility.

Michel FOUCHER (1946)

Michel Foucher, who holds a doctorate in geography, has taught at Lumière-Lyon 2 University, at the College of Europe (Warsaw campus) and at the *École Normale Supérieure* (ENS; Ulm campus). Having founded the European Geopolitical Observatory in 1987, he remained at its helm until 1998. From 2009 to 2013, he was Director of Studies at IHEDN, France's Institute for Higher National Defense Studies.

A geographer specializing in borders and national minorities, he submitted his thesis on the issue of borders in third-world countries in 1986, before becoming a permanent consultant to the French Ministry of Foreign Affairs at its Policy Planning Staff (CAP). In his capacity as Adviser on political and strategic matters to the Minister of Foreign Affairs, Hubert Védrine, he was the special envoy to the Balkans (1999), the Caucasus (2000) and then Director of the CAP. In 2002, he was appointed French Ambassador to Latvia, before returning to Paris in 2006 as Ambassador-at-large for European matters.

He has been a member of France's Foreign Affairs Council and advised the Peace and Security Division of the African Union Commission (Ethiopia) from 2007 to 2014; he has been Director of ASEAN's parliamentary diplomacy programme (PIC, Phnom Penh, in partnership with the French Parliament) since 2015. He has been an Advisory Board member for the Executive Course in European Studies (CHEE) at the French National School of Public Administration ENA since 2007, and has held the Chair of Applied Geopolitics at the *Collège d'Études Mondiales* (within the FMSH humanities institute) since 2014.

TESTIMONIALS

Oral Archives
Charter of Paris for a New Europe, 1990.
Interviewee: Michel Foucher
Number: AO110
Length: 01:48:41

Interview held in Lyon, 9 July 2020, with Jean-Philippe Dumas.

How did you become involved in reflection on the Charter of Paris?

As a geographer, I had been studying temporal and territorial aspects of European affairs since the mid-1980s, and had thus come to accumulate, I believe, a measure of expertise regarding border issues and national minorities, having examined how States emerged historically across the continent; processes which were seldom peaceful and always individually unique. This knowledge was to prove useful in the context of the geopolitical upheaval sparked in 1988-1989 when no less than 11,157 kilometres, by my calculations, of administrative boundaries or former borders were reclassified as international borders, with the latest of these, chronologically, being those of Kosovo, as yet incomplete. In other words, 27% of Europe's current borders. If we consider all of the Council of Europe's members, 72% of their current borders date from the twentieth and twenty-first centuries (with 19% stemming from the period 1945-1990, and 26% from the Balkan Wars and the Paris Peace Conference treaties).

Post-1989 developments, quite foreseeable if you take a long view of the continent's history – all European peoples identifying as emerging nations covet the attributes of statehood; all minorities seek security and protection, safeguards and autonomy – entailed serious risks. In the final version of the Charter of Paris, the phrase "national minorities" appears thirteen times. The word "border" is nowhere to be found, because of the ongoing German-Polish conundrum at the time. The concept of territorial integrity is mentioned three times.

Moreover, as a permanent consultant to the Ministry of Foreign Affairs Policy Planning Staff,[1] I was in contact with Jean Musitelli,[2] Diplomatic Adviser at the Élysée. He was interested in my forecasts, based on multiple field assignments, and I was interested in applied geopolitics. Hence our discussions, for example, about

---

[1] Policy Planning Staff (CAP): a think-tank within France's Ministry for Europe and Foreign Affairs. Established in 1974, it focuses on the international landscape and formulates strategic recommendations.

[2] Jean Musitelli: French diplomat, Diplomatic Adviser (1984-1989), Spokesperson for the President of the French Republic (1991-1995), Special Assistant to the Minister of Foreign Affairs (1990-1991; 1997). See AO108.

the French President's visits to countries in Central Europe, especially his visit to Poland in June 1989, the unofficial portion of which I had prepared *in situ*, in Gdansk.

What was your role with regard to the Élysée team?

President François Mitterrand was keenly aware of the risks inherent in the emancipation of peoples and nations from 1989 onward. The criticisms sometimes levelled at him over his sense of history are unwarranted. In his concluding address at the close of the Paris Summit (21 November 1990), he recalled the following: "Europe has paid a high price to learn that you cannot play with frontiers with impunity. But too many communities have experienced frontiers as the blade of a guillotine. Regarding the situation of national minorities: all of us here can foresee how much patience will be required by the societies in question, how much wisdom on the part of government leaders, in order to find, through dialogue and negotiation, satisfactory balances. Such impatience cannot be allayed by the reckonings of diplomacy alone." Tensions were already being felt in Romania's Transylvania regarding its Hungarian-speaking inhabitants, as well as in Yugoslavia and, as of 1988, in the Caucasus, with the war between Armenians and Azerbaijanis.

The work of the European Geopolitical Observatory, founded here in Lyon in 1989, with backing from a local bank, the CIC banking group's Lyonnaise de Banque, and decisive support from Jean-Louis Bianco,[3] who was Secretary General of the Élysée at the time, actually centred on mapping risk, which was of great interest to the Presidency's diplomatic team. Marc Epstein[4] once spoke of me as a shadow adviser: that sums up my role. I had no official capacity and my work was on a voluntary basis, as a devoted advocate for Europe but with a clear eye.

How did you come to be involved in drafting the Charter of Paris?

The Charter process was the province of our diplomatic services, but I had been wondering about the answers to questions such as: "What would a reorganized Europe look like?" or "Which kind of – geopolitical – arrangement of European territory is to be conceptualized and promoted?"

In my book[5] published in March 1988, I began to explore the implications of Gorbachev's idea of a "common home".[6] Although this Common European Home

---

[3] Jean-Louis Bianco: French politician, Secretary General of the Élysée (1982-1991).

[4] Marc Epstein: eminent reporter and later Chief Editor of the World section of *L'Express*.

[5] Michel Foucher, *Fronts and Frontières, un tour du monde géopolitique* (Fronts and Borders: A Tour of the Geopolitical World), Fayard, 1988 (in French).

[6] "Common home": an expression used by Mikhail Gorbachev, notably in his work *Perestroika*, in which he envisages the "common home" as an alternative to "the artificiality of the political blocs and the archaic nature of the iron curtain": https://www.cvce.eu/en/obj/mikhail_gorbachev_plea_for_a_common_home-en-93dc078a-78d8-4fed-aab7-1aeb3b1ce696.html

was a good idea in all fairness, it was nonetheless a Soviet idea, potentially designed with the ulterior motive of driving that famous wedge between Europe and the United States. Hence the theory that: "What is needed is the emergence of a new geopolitical system that could be called a Confederation of Democratic European States'."[7] Its economic foundations had already been laid: the EEC.[8] But it was devoid of any shared political doctrine, and lacked homogeneity and autonomy with regard to defence.

Obviously, the Soviet Union was there at the time, with its glacis.[9] The Confederation scenario offered a continent-wide European reconfiguration, connecting the EEC and the USSR, in a kind of modern concert of nations. The Charter of Paris for a New Europe was a step in the process, in which the end of the Cold War was acknowledged. But what next, over and above those principles?

Did you attend the Paris Summit?

For me, the Paris Summit was an extraordinary experience. I had never met Gorbachev, George Bush senior, Thatcher or Kohl. My lasting impression of that plenary meeting is one of those powerful leaders – in my upcoming book I refer to them as giants ("diri-géants") instead of leaders ("dirigeants") – who were responsible for bringing the Cold War to a close, but in a true spirit of negotiation, without striking a blow and without visible tension.

What was François Mitterrand's vision for Europe?

That earlier quote from Mitterrand sums it up. To his mind, regained freedom was a mighty prize, but it could come at a high cost if nationalist forces, long held in check by the communist regimes, were to break loose. Hence his insistence on establishing lasting institutions, and on laying down principles and rules, especially with regard to national minorities and territorial integrity.

The role of the Council of Europe[10] had likely been underestimated in Paris. And then there was the failure of the Prague Confederation Conference (June 1991). The Confederation project came too early – the Soviet Union was still there – and the United States, still busy extending its hegemony by offering security guarantees to Moscow's former satellite countries, wouldn't hear of it. And it peddled the idea

---

[7] Op. cit., 1st edition, page 422 (in French).
[8] European Economic Community (EEC): a supranational organization instituted by the Treaty of Rome in 1957.
[9] Glacis: meaning the USSR's satellite States between NATO and the USSR.
[10] Council of Europe: intergovernmental organization encompassing 47 countries, instituted by the Treaty of London (1949), promoting the rule of law and democratic principles in Europe.

that France was pushing for a Confederation so as to postpone EEC accession for the Central European and Baltic countries, a process which actually went on to take some fifteen years anyway (1989-2004/2007)!

The Confederation never came into being, but was there any follow-up to it?

It was later, as I was writing *Atlas de l'influence française au XXIᵉ siècle* (Atlas of French Influence in the 21st Century),[11] that I came to the conclusion that our influence was, and remains, connected to our ability to produce ideas, provided they can be implemented with others. The Confederation idea was one of these. The ideas have not gone away: what let them down were the structures, the mechanisms, in a context of Western hubris. And the question of European concert, of Russia's place in Europe, that nagging question that has hounded European geopolitics for at least the last two centuries, is still being asked. But not answered.

Édouard Balladur[12] had grasped the need for a stability pact, linking Central European countries' progress toward EEC accession with prior settlement of border issues and of national minorities' status. Sophie-Caroline de Margerie,[13] at the behest of Hubert Védrine, had quizzed me on all of these issues so as to verify them before being able to validate the Balladur Plan. I can still remember her comment at the end of our discussion on "the absoluteness of borders". The Balladur Plan had set forth a conditionality, which was operational a few years after 1990 but in accordance with the Charter's principles: that the path to Brussels necessarily included stopovers in three cities: Bucharest, Budapest and Bratislava.

Did France's leaders feel that the CSCE and the Confederation were in competition with one another?

It could be interpreted that way, yes. The Germans were focused on the CSCE, their protection, during negotiations with Moscow on crucial considerations: withdrawal of Red Army troops, reunification and the end of the GDR sister regime, etc. From France's perspective, the drawback of the CSCE was that it involved the Americans and the EEC, which was above all an economic institution, was not designed for such rapid expansion; the idea, rather, was to come up with a new framework in which to address political and legal matters, borders and minorities, rule of law and human rights, as well as cultural and physical exchanges. Mitterrand held these key aspects very dear. The solution was the expansion of NATO. Remember that the Central European and Baltic states joined NATO a few weeks prior to entering the

---

[11] Published by Robert Laffont, 2013 (in French). The book's findings were presented at the 2013 Ambassadors' Conference on influence.

[12] Édouard Balladur: French statesman, Prime Minister (1993-1995).

[13] Sophie-Caroline de Margerie: French diplomat, European Affairs Adviser to the French Presidency (1988-1992). See AO109.

Discussion between Edouard Chevardnadze and Roland Dumas in the Conference Centre at the Ministry of Foreign Affairs, avenue Kléber, 19 November 1990.

European Union (1 May 2004), a symbol of reaffirmed American leadership. That did not exactly square with the French vision of a truly autonomous Europe, organizing its own affairs as it saw fit.

How did you feel about the involvement of the Americans?

The Americans had pressured the Central European countries to join the EU, guaranteeing their security, while leaving the Europeans to take charge of economic development, while menacingly drumming the leitmotiv, if negotiations ever got stuck, of a new "division of Europe, an economic division". Admittedly, accession required a lot of preparation whereas fulfilment of NATO's admission criteria occurred after entry.

Today, the intangibility of borders is deemed one of the Charter of Paris's great achievements.

Yes, but the cardinal legal principle is the inviolability of borders. Borders are not intangible if they can be changed by common accord. In an interview with the

Frankfurter Allgemeine Zeitung, Mitterrand stated that internal administrative boundaries could be changed and become international borders, particularly in former federations. If a line is shifted by force, as in Ukraine's Donbass region or in northern Georgia, then it is an act of war, a breach of international law. The philosopher Hegel once wrote that waging war meant letting your border ramble into someone else's territory.

What was envisaged for the economy, alongside the Charter of Paris?

The EEC took on its economic programme. Very early on – in 1989 – France had proposed, through Élisabeth Guigou,[14] assistance mechanisms for the upcoming political and economic transition, with the PHARE programme (Poland and Hungary: Assistance for the Restructuring of the Economy). The Hungarians were the first to benefit from it because theirs was the most modern of the socialist economies. Economic aspects were taken into consideration, as were energy and environmental issues: two key areas of the Confederation scenario that were discussed in Prague. We need to acknowledge that these aspects, foremost in everyone's minds today, are making slow progress. I get the feeling that the European Commission adopted the key concepts identified in 1990 at the Paris Summit, with prudent blessings expressed in Prague.

What is still missing is a multinational European structure enabling practical cooperation across the entire continent among the EU's member States and those countries that are not, and never will be, members. Moscow still tends to think in terms of post-imperial spheres of influence. In the words of Frédéric Petit, French National Assembly Deputy for the 7th Constituency of French Nationals Abroad, and member of the Foreign Affairs Commission,[15] concerning the political crisis in Belarus: "The European Union should have clear, comprehensible borders, defended by Europeans, stretching from Lisbon to Varna to Copenhagen; and beyond these clarified, accepted borders, which are both physically and symbolically strong, we should stop fantasizing about dilutive and unrealistic enlargements, and instead develop a genuine 'neighbourhood policy' which could thus be truly balanced, a source of sovereignty and progress. It could serve as an inspiration to our 'neighbours', as we have just seen in the case of Belarus. It would facilitate 'good relations' based not only on economic ties, but also on culture and on the recognition of latent, forgotten, or painful narratives." After the Charter of Paris, a federal scenario would offer a suitable framework: food for diplomatic thought.

---

[14] Élisabeth Guigou: French politician, Secretary-General of the Inter-Ministerial Committee on Economic Aspects of European Cooperation (1985-1990), Minister Delegate for European Affairs (1990-1993).

[15] *Que nous apprend la crise politique au sujet de la Bélarus et de l'Union européenne ?* (What Lessons from the Political Crisis regarding Belarus and the European Union?) 19 August 2020, Petit/Diploweb (in French).

Marc PERRIN DE BRICHAMBAUT (1948)

Marc Perrin de Brichambaut is an alumnus of the *École Normale Supérieure de Saint-Cloud* and, having graduated from the Paris Institute of Political Studies and obtained his *agrégation* teaching qualification in geography, he opted for the *Conseil d'État* when he left France's National School of Public Administration (ENA) in 1974 ("Simone Weil" year).

In 1978, he left for New York to take up the post of Special Assistant to the United Nations Under-Secretary-General for International Economic and Social Affairs. Upon his return to Paris in 1981, he became the Technical Adviser on International Economic Affairs and Development to the Minister of External Relations, Claude Cheysson. In 1984, Roland Dumas, Minister of Foreign Affairs, appointed him Deputy Director and then Director of his Private Office. He was posted again to New York in 1986 as the Embassy's Cultural Counsellor and permanent representative of French universities to the United States.

In June 1988, he was appointed Diplomatic Adviser to the Minister of Defence, Jean-Pierre Chevènement. It was in this capacity that he worked on the negotiations leading to the Treaty on Conventional Armed Forces in Europe. He returned to the Ministry of Foreign Affairs in the summer of 1991 as an Ambassador, representing France in Vienna at the negotiations on conventional armed forces and on confidence- and security-building measures in Europe. In 1994, he returned to the Central Administration as Legal Affairs Director. In this role he led the French delegation in the Rome Statute negotiations of the International Criminal Court.

In 1998, he was designated to join the Permanent Court of Arbitration in The Hague. In parallel, he was Strategic Affairs Director at the Ministry of Defence until 2005, when he was appointed Secretary General of the OSCE in Vienna, an office he held until 2011.

Since 2015, he has been a judge at the International Criminal Court. The opinions expressed in this interview in no way reflect the position of said institution.

MARC PERRIN DE BRICHAMBAUT

Oral Archives
Charter of Paris for a New Europe, 1990.
Interviewee: Marc Perrin de Brichambaut
Number: AO112
Length: 00:58:41

Interview dated 22 July 2020, with Nicolas Badalassi and Jean-Philippe Dumas.

How were you involved in the preparation of the Paris Summit held in November 1990?

I should first of all like to paint the backdrop. At the time I was Diplomatic Adviser to the Minister of Defence, Jean-Pierre Chevènement,[1] and the two years leading up to November 1990 were, with regard to France's security interests, largely dominated by the negotiations on the treaty on conventional armed forces in Europe.[2] The Treaty on Conventional Armed Forces in Europe (CFE) was signed the day before the Paris Summit opened by the member States of NATO and those of the Warsaw Pact. The United States had set the adoption of this Treaty as a precondition for their participation in the Paris Summit that was to adopt the Charter.

This Treaty was the culmination of a tremendous amount of work, since it entailed establishing agreed ceilings for armaments held by the Treaty's States Parties across five categories of equipment, and identifying their location, with a view to preventing any surprise attacks, and undertaking reciprocal verification of the destruction of excess equipment. At that time, the Warsaw Pact[3] was still in force, and therefore the commitments made under the Treaty on Conventional Armed Forces in Europe concerned both the members of the Pact and those of NATO in interlocking areas. It was a complex arrangement that had been negotiated at the highest level. I had accompanied the Minister of Defence to Moscow in the months preceding the conclusion of these talks. The text of the Treaty was finalized in Vienna in negotiations where Ambassador François Plaisant represented France.

My participation in the Charter process was thus indirect and in parallel, because we, in the Ministry of Defence, were working very closely with the Ministry

---

[1] Jean-Pierre Chevènement: French senior official and politician, Minister of Defence (1988-1991).

[2] *Treaty on Conventional Armed Forces in Europe*: The *Mutual and Balanced Force Reductions* (MBFR) talks were a series of negotiations held in Vienna between the North Atlantic Treaty Organization (NATO) and the Warsaw Pact, between 1973 and 1989, aiming to foster disarmament and control conventional weapons in the FRG, the GDR, Benelux, Czechoslovakia and Poland. In 1990, the MBFR was replaced by the *Treaty on Conventional Armed Forces in Europe*, which set new armament limits after the end of the Cold War.

[3] Warsaw Pact: a military alliance formed on 14 May 1955 bringing the countries of Eastern Europe and the USSR together in an economic, political and military group. The alliance was dissolved in July 1991.

of Foreign Affairs. I was present when the Treaty was signed, just one day before that Summit that adopted the Charter of Paris. It was a significant event because it made it possible to move on from the confrontation of two very sizeable ensembles of armed forces, unprecedented in history, that were present on European soil, and to seek a situation of new trust. A document on confidence-building measures among the different States of Europe including, above and beyond the States Parties to the CFE Treaty, the neutral and non-aligned countries, was to be subsequently negotiated and adopted. It was called the Vienna Document on confidence- and security-building measures, and it rounded off the security provisions of the post-Helsinki[4] world.

It was in this way that I was able to personally observe the Summit deliberations. I was authorized to attend in the conference room itself, which had been built in a great hurry and which spilled out over Avenue Kléber. The building was later destroyed. It was a striking occasion because it was possible to see the various heads of State and government around the table: Bush, Gorbachev, Mrs Thatcher, Kohl and Mitterrand. If my memory serves me correctly, the general debate was not so different from any other of its genre. The thirty-five heads of State and government were each allotted a speaking time of ten minutes at the most. Some respected the time limit; others ran over, while the others either listened politely or did something else, such as reading the newspaper or conversing with their colleagues. In reality, all of the groundwork for this kind of multilateral meeting is conducted on the margins of the plenary and is, as far as possible, stitched up before the meeting opens.

You also participated directly in the implementation of the Charter.

I was indeed involved, as of June 1991, representing France in the Vienna negotiations, in the implementation of the Charter's provisions, in all their fullness and complexity, including in the implementation of the various decisions regarding the establishment of institutional mechanisms.

You will recall that the Charter created four institutions. The precise role of the Secretariat in Prague had yet to be properly identified and its functions remained unclear; the Conflict Prevention Centre was in Vienna; while the Office for Democratic Institutions and Human Rights was to be subsequently located in Warsaw. Getting these institutions up and running involved a tremendous amount of work, which was all undertaken at a time when events in the former Yugoslavia were spiralling out of control.[5] This regional crisis, which emerged first in Slovenia, then in

---

[4] Helsinki Final Act (1975): document comprising mutual commitments regarding security in Europe, human rights and intergovernmental cooperation.

[5] Conflicts in the former Yugoslavia: in December 1990, Croatia and Slovenia officially proclaimed the pro-independence referendum results, and issued an ultimatum to the Yugoslav authorities the following month, leading to intervention by federal troops, controlled by Serbia.

Croatia, therefore had to be factored into the implementation of the Charter of Paris. Seen from Vienna, the obvious question was that of identifying the framework in which to try to stabilize this swiftly developing crisis. The CSCE[6] was initially viewed as a potential framework for enabling direct involvement in handling the crisis. I distinctly remember several discussions in which my colleagues were left perplexed at the idea of creating a genuine peacekeeping operation under the aegis of the CSCE when it was still in the structuring process. There was a marked lack of enthusiasm for this idea from my interlocutors. And then things started taking a rapid turn for the worse, and the CSCE option was ruled out in favour of a United Nations option. Consideration was nonetheless given to giving the WEU a potential maritime role.

In the first six months of my tenure in Vienna as of July 1991, much of my time was taken up with preparations for the CSCE Ministerial Council and the Helsinki Summit. On that occasion, the preparatory meetings for the ministerial conference ahead of the Helsinki Summit of July 1992 lasted well-nigh three months and took place at the location of the conference. The French delegation in Helsinki was spearheaded by Ambassador Yves Pagniez. The delegation played a proactive role in fine-tuning the texts adopted to establish the practical and institutional mechanisms very present in the Charter of Paris. But the events taking place in the former Yugoslavia and Iraq formed an ominous backdrop to deliberations at the Ministerial Council, and then at the Summit.

This was thus the period in which many of the Charter's provisions were implemented and its institutions were formed. And it was in Stockholm, in September 1992, during the CSCE Ministerial Council, that there was a decision to give the CSCE a Secretary General. I vividly recall Roland Dumas[7] handing me a German diplomat's card and asking me: "For Secretary General, what do you think?" The name on the card was that of Wilhelm Hoynck,[8] who became the CSCE's first Secretary General; a very distinguished gentleman, who endeavoured to give substance to a rather complicated function, rather difficult to put into effect.

While you were busy with the implementation of the Paris Summit decisions, the Americans were pushing for an expansion of NATO.

It nevertheless required a prolonged period of reflection at the White House, followed by negotiations with the other stakeholders in Washington, before the United States Senate agreed to this prospect of expanding NATO. It took more than

---

[6] CSCE: Conference on Security and Co-operation in Europe; a forum for negotiation between the two Cold War blocs, active from 1973 until 1994. The Helsinki Final Act (1975) emanated from the CSCE.

[7] Roland Dumas: French politician, Minister of Foreign Affairs from 1988 to 1993.

[8] Wilhelm Hoynck: German diplomat, Secretary General of the OSCE from 1993 to 1996.

Signature of the Treaty on Conventional Armed Forces in Europe (CFE), at the Élysée Palace, on 19 November 1990.
From left to right: George H. W. Bush, Hans-Dietrich Genscher, Helmut Kohl, Roland Dumas, Michel Rocard, François Mitterrand, Edouard Chevardnadze, Mikhail Gorbatchev.

> The signature of the CFE Treaty by the representatives of NATO Member States and Warsaw Pact Member States is the first event of the Paris Summit. The FCE Treaty aims to considerably reduce conventional arms while maintaining balanced deterrence.

two years for the Clinton administration – over and above all the turmoil in Yugoslavia – to agree to appear before the Senate and appeal for the first three Eastern European States to join NATO. And this was possible only after methodical simultaneous lobbying by two highly talented lobbyists, Bruce Jackson[9] for the Republicans, and Ronald Asmus[10] for the Democrats: they created a committee advocating NATO

---

[9] Bruce Jackson: Military Intelligence Officer in the US Army, who served in the Office of the Secretary of Defence on arms control and defence strategy from 1986 to 1990.

[10] Ronald D. Asmus: United States diplomat.

expansion, and systematically lobbied each and every Senator. Some Senators were averse to the idea of NATO expanding the scope of its security responsibilities to include new States. At the time, there were many in Washington and elsewhere saying: "You know, we have to be careful with the Russians" and similar such comments.

For a time, at least up until the CSCE Summit in Budapest[11] – which François Mitterrand attended in November 1994 and which saw the CSCE become the OSCE –, there was still hope for the prospect of an ambitious European security architecture. Germany's Foreign Minister, Hans-Dietrich Genscher, set great store by it and enjoyed a privileged relationship with his French counterpart, Roland Dumas. During this period, numerous high-level meetings were held, further underpinning the role played by the Charter of Paris as a platform for both conflict prevention and humanistic concerns, resulting in major breakthroughs in Copenhagen, Moscow and Vienna. In the course of regular consultations, Vienna witnessed the adoption not only of the Vienna Document on confidence-building measures, binding on all CSCE States, but also the Open Skies Treaty.

But the pan-European perspective began to change from the moment that the first NATO enlargement started taking shape. A sort of backlash could be felt from the Russians, which intensified and grew once President Yeltsin's successor, Vladimir Putin, came to power: while President Putin appeared to view the OSCE quite favourably at the start of his first term, by 2007 he was to refer to it as a "vulgarny instrument" at the Munich Conference.

Throughout this period, the OSCE was perceived as an instrument of pan-European security where Russia and the States closely connected to it stood on an equal footing with their partners. It remained the instrument of choice for Soviet Russian diplomacy. It was an extension of the "common home" concept mooted by Gorbachev, which reprised an old Soviet idea, bandied about even before the 1975 meeting in Helsinki. Over the years, the only Minister of Foreign Affairs to have been present over the two days of each annual Ministerial Council at the OSCE is Sergey Lavrov.[12] I was in regular contact with him when I was Secretary General of the OSCE. My Russian contacts would tell me: "When Lavrov arrives in the office each morning, the first thing that he looks at are two batches of telegrams: the ones from the United Nations, and those from the OSCE."

---

[11] Budapest Summit (5-6 December 1994): A summit that concluded with the Declaration intitled "Towards a Genuine Partnership in a New Era" enshrining the name change from CSCE to OSCE.

[12] Sergey Lavrov: Russian diplomat and politician, Director of the Foreign Ministry's Department for International Organizations and Global Affairs from 1990 to 1992, then Vice-Minister of Foreign Affairs of the Russian Federation from 1992 to 1994.

Could the Charter of Paris have been implemented differently?

Grand statements of principles like the Charter of Paris can only ever truly be put into practice if all key partners pledge their intense, thorough, and sustainable political commitment to it. And even then, the circumstances and context need to be propitious. If it had not been for the events in the former Yugoslavia, the Charter of Paris might have become the matrix, in some ways, of a new order of cooperative security in Europe, serving as a framework for other organizations. But Yugoslavia cropped up, a number of other events cropped up, not to mention Eastern European peoples' aspiration to return to the European family's fold, for which NATO stood as a powerful symbol. Joining the European Union came second; immediately afterwards.

Later, after the second NATO enlargement, President Bush's ambition of bringing Ukraine and Georgia into NATO undermined whatever minimum consensus there may have been with regard to the OSCE as of 2007. The atmosphere became uncomfortable in Vienna after the war in Georgia in August 2008. It is thus important to take a step back and take a long-term view of things in order to understand the fate of the Charter of Paris.

In terms of security, could the Charter have been applied differently?

If there is something truly original about the Charter of Paris it is the affirmation of the multi-dimensional nature of security, as expressed in the Helsinki Decalogue,[13] adopted in 1975. The Charter takes this idea further, explicitly identifying what those different dimensions entail, and at the same time it broadens the scope of some existing domains and addresses new domains. This represents an overarching ambition of the CSCE-OSCE process: the idea of working in parallel and making progress in each of the different baskets, which have developed into the different axes of the OSCE's work, and simultaneously making advances in all of the constituent aspects of security. Security is thus based on a sort of consistency, or convergence, among these different mutually reinforcing domains. This is a tough task, by definition, both conceptually and diplomatically. It provides a strong, fair framework for analysis, but is difficult to actually put into action with the various instruments created in the CSCE-OSCE toolkit. The OSCE field missions, which commenced in 1993, aimed to horizontally combine the different dimensions of security, by furthering the rule of law, private sector development, police reform, reforms of the courts and environmental protection; all of this with only modest means and limited leverage.

---

[13] The Decalogue: the ten principles governing reciprocal relations among States participating in the CSCE, established at the 1975 Helsinki Summit.

One aspect that has always been of primary importance in the wake of the Charter of Paris is the implementation of existing texts on arms control and confidence-building measures. It comes in the form of ongoing dialogue on security through regular consultations at the Forum for Security Co-operation in Vienna. Another post-Charter area of work involves the CSE-OSCE's handling of a number of conflicts, notably the so-called "frozen" conflicts stemming from the breakup of the Soviet Union in Nagorno-Karabakh,[14] in Transnistria,[15] in Abkhazia[16] and in South Ossetia.[17]

Implementing the Charter's security aspirations is therefore a multi-faceted endeavour requiring tenacious political will and careful monitoring by all stakeholders involved. It is a complicated task, and one that still has pride of place on the OSCE's agenda today. This approach has been imitated in other fora, for other situations, and is becoming widespread.

How does the OSCE operate today?

What sets the CSCE-OSCE process apart is that its primary responsibility emanates from the Chairperson-in-Office. Each year, one State takes over the Chair, which is a most demanding task. This responsibility means deploying a good dozen diplomats for duty in Vienna as well as a solid team back in the capital. It involves designating a whole range of special representatives and considerable efforts for preparation and training, with support from the Organization's permanent secretariat and Secretary General.

The political benefits of this work are not always immediately obvious to the country performing it. But it does enable the small or medium-sized States to demonstrate their contribution to stability in Europe and their acceptance of the sacrifices and vagaries inherent in the task. More often than not, the Minister of Foreign Affairs launching the process is not in fact the one who subsequently handles it, as the post tends to change hands in the meantime. The Minister who serves as Chairperson-in-Office needs to dedicate considerable time to the duties of the Chair, but this opens access to every major capital. Holding the Chair also means taking charge of the annual Ministerial Council. Since the Istanbul Summit of 1999,[18] conditions

---

[14] Nagorno-Karabakh: separatist region of chiefly Armenian ethnicity which had been part of Soviet Azerbaijan, and which was at the centre of a war between 1988 and 1994.

[15] Transnistria: region located between Ukraine and Moldova, over which there was armed conflict between pro-Transnistrian and pro-Moldovan forces from November 1990 until the ceasefire of July 1992.

[16] Abkhazia: region in Georgia. From 1992 to 1993, it was the site of armed conflict between Russian Federation forces and Abkhaz separatists on the one hand, and Georgian troops on the other.

[17] South Ossetia: breakaway region that seceded from Georgia in 1992, declaring itself an independent Republic.

[18] Istanbul Summit: Summit attended by OSCE member States, 18-19 November 1999.

Visit to Sweden by Roland Dumas for the meeting of the CSCE Council of Ministers, 14-15 December 1992. *On the left*, Margaretha Af Ugglas, Sweden's Minister for Foreign Affairs.

In Stockholm, CSCE Participating States decide on the creation of a Secretariat-General for the organization of regular meetings in Vienna.

were such that it was not always possible to hold regular summits as stipulated in the Charter of Paris. It was not until there was a Kazakh Chair, with the concomitant energetic personal commitment from President Nazarbayev, that a new Summit could be held, in Astana in 2010.

Over and above the Ministerial Councils and the Summits, the countries are all represented in Vienna by Ambassadors who meet several times a week. They are professionals in multilateral diplomacy and the topics discussed at their meetings make it possible to take the temperature of relations across greater Europe. While the exchanges may sometimes be heated and full of tension, the channels of communication are kept continuously open. In this regard, the Charter's legacy continues thanks to the existence of a permanent consultation framework where a wide range of topics are addressed around a central focus: common security. The OSCE embodies the continuity of the only pan-European security entity where there is ongoing dialogue on an equal footing among all of the States in great Europe. This is important for Russia and numerous other countries who are not members of NATO or the

EU such as those in the Balkans, the Caucasus or Central Asia. The OSCE furthermore maintains intense dialogue on all of these dimensions with its Mediterranean and Asian partners.

Each of the OSCE family's three institutions, the Office for Democratic Institutions and Human Rights, the High-Commissioner on National Minorities and the Representative on Freedom of the Media, plays an important complementary role in its respective dimension. The same is true for field missions which, upon the invitation of the host country, help promote OSCE values in a dozen or so States Parties.

What was Jean-Pierre Chevènement's personal contribution to this process?

Jean-Pierre Chevènement, being such a dedicated French politician, was always one of the more enthusiastic proponents of a pan-European security architecture, and one of the more willing to work on this issue with any interlocutors that he could find, be they Russian or German. His analyses on these matters were always perfectly cogent. He was an active participant in discussions among François Mitterrand's entourage in the pivotal post-Cold War years. It was he who implemented the major orientations determined by the French President himself. I remember having a conversation with him when, as Minister of Defence, he had just returned from stating his case at the Élysée Palace, and being asked to supply him with notes and files so that he could pursue his dialogue with the President.

The Americans were not easy interlocutors: they had their own ideas, and weighed in heavily on the 2+4 consultations regarding Germany's reunification. The years 1989 and 1990 were a period of intense diplomatic exchanges and several crises were unfolding at the same time as German reunification and the future of security in Europe were under discussion. France was fortunate to have had leaders endowed with vast intellectual capacity and a heightened sense of statesmanship: François Mitterrand, Roland Dumas, and Jean-Pierre Chevènement. Their work served the interests of France and shaped the new face of Europe.

The Charter of Paris is one of the avenues explored in the process of identifying the framework of great Europe. It is but one of several projects that emerged at a given point in time. It made a truly significant contribution but was not the only model. It engendered a very fertile process that became blended with other inspirations. Discussions are far from over, and the Charter remains a source of inspiration and an incomparable guide for action both in Europe and beyond.

Lucien CHAMPENOIS (1933)

Having graduated from INALCO (National Institute for Oriental Languages and Civilizations) in Arabic and Persian, Lucien Champenois joined the Ministry of Foreign Affairs in 1960 and took up his first posting at the French Embassy in Rabat. This was followed by Jeddah, and then Bern, before his return to Morocco in the late 1960s. In 1971, he joined the Directorate-General for Cultural, Scientific and Technical Relations, and then in 1975, moved to the Economic and Financial Affairs Directorate. After a three-year period working at the Ministry of Industry, Commerce and Trades (1977-1980), he returned to cultural relations. In 1982, he was Head of the Development Projects Department in the Ministry of Cooperation, before becoming the Technical Adviser to the Director of Development Policy (1984-1986). He later joined the French Embassy in the Holy See as First Counsellor.

Upon his return to Paris in September 1989, he was posted to the Europe Directorate, as Special Assistant on the CSCE to Jacques Blot. He subsequently took over as head of the CSCE Unit in Paris, as of 1991, and coordinated all of the French delegations' work. He thus participated in various CSCE Meetings of Experts, such as those held in Sofia, Valetta, Bonn, Copenhagen, Geneva and Krakow. Following the creation of permanent institutions by the Charter of Paris, he represented France on several occasions at the Committee of Senior Officials. He attended the Helsinki Summit in July 1992, before being appointed Adviser on Religious Affairs at the Ministry of Foreign Affairs (1992-1998).

LUCIEN CHAMPENOIS

Oral Archives
Charter of Paris for a New Europe, 1990.
Interviewee: Lucien Champenois
Number: AO113
Length: 01:01:04

How did you become involved with the CSCE and the drafting of the Charter of Paris?

In October 1989, I took up my post as Special Assistant on the CSCE[1] to the Europe Director, Jacques Blot,[2] and I went to see the then Political Affairs Director, Bertrand Dufourcq.[3] A few weeks later, I went to Sofia to attend a meeting of environmental experts[4] and this was my introduction to the workings of the CSCE, and the moment when I witnessed the first cracks heralding the ultimate collapse of the Soviet bloc.

I must pay tribute to the skill and commitment of my deputy at the time, Gérard Fauveau,[5] who thoroughly briefed me on the CSCE process, which was an ensemble of clever procedures whose cornerstone was the rule of consensus. The advantage of this conception of the process was that it avoided the creation of permanent structures, thus affording the possibility of stopping at any time if there was no way forward. The obvious drawback was that there would be no way forward at all unless relations between the blocs were relatively calm; if things were too tense, everything would inevitably grind to a halt.

How did the Charter of Paris fit in with the CSCE process?

Due to the GDR's disintegration, which caught short each chancellery, and after the free elections of March 1990, won by the proponents of Germany's reunification,[6] the new East-German Parliament voted for reunification with effect as of 3 October 1990.

---

[1] Conference on Security and Co-operation in Europe (CSCE): a forum for negotiation between the two Cold War blocs, active from 1973 until 1994.

[2] Jacques Blot: French diplomat, Europe Director from 1987 to 1992.

[3] Bertrand Dufourcq: French diplomat, Ambassador to Russia from 1990 to 1992, then to Germany 1992-1993, and Secretary-General at Quai d'Orsay from 1993 to 1998. He took part in the 2+4 treaty negotiations on Germany's reunification in 1990, when he was Quai d'Orsay's Political Affairs Director.

[4] CSCE Meeting on the Protection of the Environment in Sofia (16 October to 3 November 1989).

[5] Gérard Fauveau: French diplomat, present at the conference on disarmament in Europe, in Stockholm (February 1985 to September 1986); CSCE in Vienna from 1986 to 1989; Europe Directorate from 1989 to 1991.

[6] Reunification: process enabling the union of the two parts of partitioned Germany into one State. Occurring between 1989 and 1990, Germany's reunification entailed the FRG's absorption of the GDR.

It was in this context that a meeting of Heads of State and Government was convened for all of the CSCE's participating States, to be held in Paris, 19-21 November 1990, so as to adopt the Charter of Paris for a New Europe. There was clearly a desire to reiterate the principles that had guided the creation of the CSCE, but also to usher in a new era in relations among its participating States – and hopefully make further progress.

Anyone reading the Charter will immediately notice that this mood is reflected in the somewhat triumphalist style – I was aware of it at the time, but I find it even more striking now – highlighting the success of Western democratic values, which were thenceforth expected to guide participating States' domestic and foreign policies. And the participating States undertook to build and strengthen democracy as their nations' only system of government.

Within this framework are set out the legitimate rights and freedoms of individuals. Immediately following the section on freedoms comes an elaboration on "Economic Liberty and Responsibility", which sets forth, among other objectives for the participating States, the aim of developing market economies, while being careful to stipulate they these are to go hand in hand with social justice and respect for the environment.

Curiously, it is only after the above considerations that the major peace and security problems are addressed, with reference to the Ten Principles of the 1975 Helsinki Final Act[7] and those of the Charter of the United Nations,[8] including the pledge to refrain from the threat or use of force against the territorial integrity or political independence of any State. Equal rights of peoples and their right to self-determination are also reaffirmed, in conformity with the Charter of the United Nations and with relevant norms of international law.

Under the "Security" heading, the participating States welcome the signature by twenty-two participating States of the Treaty on Conventional Armed Forces in Europe,[9] which aimed to achieve unprecedented reductions in armed forces in

---

[7] The Ten Principles of the Helsinki Final Act offer security guarantees to States: sovereign equality, refraining from the threat or use of force, inviolability of frontiers, respect for territorial integrity, peaceful settlement of disputes, non-intervention in the internal affairs of States, respect for human rights and fundamental freedoms, equality and self-determination of peoples, cooperation among States, fulfilment in good faith of international obligations.

[8] Charter of the United Nations or Charter of San Francisco: sets forth the principles of the UN and how it works.

[9] *Treaty on Conventional Armed Forces in Europe*: The *Mutual and Balanced Force Reductions* (MBFR) talks were a series of negotiations held in Vienna between the North Atlantic Treaty Organization (NATO) and the Warsaw Pact, between 1973 and 1989, aiming to foster disarmament and control conventional weapons in the FRG, the GDR, Benelux, Czechoslovakia and Poland. In 1990, the MBFR was replaced by the *Treaty on Conventional Armed Forces in Europe*, which established new armament limits after the end of the Cold War.

Europe. These 22 States comprised 16 + 7, meaning the 16 member States of NATO[10] + 7, but the seven were reduced to six as the GDR was integrated into the Federal Republic of Germany.

Finally, in the "Unity" section, the participating States note with great satisfaction the Treaty on the Final Settlement with Respect to Germany,[11] considering that achieving Germany's national unity is an "important contribution to a just and lasting order of peace for a united, democratic Europe..." which is obviously an elegant solution to the problem of the peace treaties that Germany ought to have signed successively with each State with which it had been at war.

After these vast doctrinal developments, the Charter of Paris addressed what would ultimately be a fundamental turning point for the CSCE: the creation of its permanent institutions. The CSCE was no longer a process, but an international organization. A few years later, incidentally, in 1995, it took on a new name reflecting this change: the OSCE, or Organization for Security and Co-operation in Europe.

The governing body of the Organization is the Ministerial Council, made up of Ministers of Foreign Affairs, which meets at least once a year. Its work is prepared by a committee of senior officials who then oversee the implementation of the Council's decisions. A Secretariat was created in Prague for the administrative support of these structures, and two other bodies were established: a Conflict Prevention Centre[12] based in Vienna and an Office for Free Elections based in Warsaw. The latter would later have its functions expanded to become the Office for Democratic Institutions and Human Rights, the French acronym of which, BIDDH, elicits the odd snigger... And the meetings of Heads of State and Government, or follow-up meetings to the Summits in Helsinki, 1975, and in Paris, would theoretically take place every two years.

Significantly, to my mind, the setting for the very first Ministerial Council was Berlin, on 19 and 20 June 1991. The effects of the shock triggered by Germany's reunification were thus plainly visible. As it transpired, this date coincided with the Bundestag's vote in Bonn on moving the capital of the Federal Republic from Bonn to Berlin. This was a vexed issue, the subject of heated debates in Bonn itself, within the German Parliament, and was adopted by 337 votes to 320. This might be a clear margin, but it is not an overly large one.

---

[10] North Atlantic Treaty Organization (NATO): the organization implementing the politico-military alliance between the United States and Western Europe. Designed to ensure security against the Soviet bloc, it was founded in 1949 at the outset of the Cold War.

[11] Treaty on the Final Settlement with Respect to Germany (1990): also known as the Moscow Treaty or the 2+4 Treaty (the two German States plus the four occupying powers: the United States, France, the United Kingdom and the USSR).

[12] Conflict Prevention Centre (CPC): the OSCE's warning mechanism designed to prevent conflict and foster mediation attempts.

What was the Paris Summit like?

From the outset the idea was to make it as spectacular as possible and imaginable. Truly remarkable work had been carried out to upgrade the Conference Centre on rue La Pérouse. Temporary buildings had been constructed. I recall that when the plenary session for Heads of State and Government opened, those who were attending as spectators like me were sitting in darkness. All of a sudden, the lights came on and we saw before us this assembly of Heads of State and Government. It was quite spectacular. I also remember that the person whose presence made the biggest impression on me was Margaret Thatcher, as she simply radiated energy. She really was a quite an extraordinary person in terms of temperament.

I did not have a direct hand in the preparations for the Paris Summit, but I did attend the Meetings of Experts that preceded it, the Bonn meeting on economic cooperation, the meeting in Copenhagen and the second one on the Human Dimension.

Could you tell us about these Meetings of Experts, which are the hallmark of the CSCE?

I took part in many meetings, notably the one in Valetta, which was on the peaceful settlement of disputes, from 15 January to 8 February 1991, and the one in Krakow on cultural heritage.[13] The interests at stake in both were obviously quite different.

At the Valetta conference, there was one State in particular that had its sights firmly on a certain project, and that was Switzerland. The Swiss delegate had devised a project, quite a well-fleshed-out system, and gave us all some undeniably interesting presentations about the different dispute-resolution mechanisms from negotiation to mediation to good offices. There were escalating levels all the way up to arbitration, which was mandatory. And he had developed a mechanism which he wanted to be made binding. While everybody was in perfect agreement that the project certainly displayed many fine qualities, nobody in the room had the slightest appetite for a binding system. So our discussions continued, and we came up with a document that, although worthwhile, insofar as it examined the various possible forms of negotiations for resolving disputes peacefully, was not at all binding. What really struck me at that moment was the noticeable disarray in the Soviet delegation, which was manifested in its contradictory positions. The overall atmosphere was also strange owing to the imminent American intervention in Iraq, which loomed large in everyone's minds.

In Krakow, a city full of charm, with its exceptionally interesting, exceptionally beautiful architecture, our discussions in the Meeting of Experts – or at least

---

[13] CSCE Krakow meeting: colloquium on cultural heritage, from 28 May to 7 June 1991.

the opening and closing sessions – were conducted in the Krakow theatre, which is a gem of eighteenth-century architecture. All the dignitaries were assembled on the balcony seats, including Macharski, the Cardinal and Archbishop of Krakow.[14] A rather tragicomic episode then ensued: The Foreign Minister from the new Polish government – the first after the Polish People's Republic – launched into a diatribe that was clearly directed at Moscow, but in veiled terms. Upon hearing this, the Russian delegate rose to his feet, and I don't recall his exact words, but he was essentially saying: "Even so, let us not forget all those who gave their lives in the Red Army to liberate you." And he requested a minute's silence in their memory, which is not customary at all in CSCE procedure. But in the end, everyone respected the minute of silence.

There was another episode that I remember: I was offered a choice of several excursions. There was a weekend in the middle of the conference, and so our Polish hosts had arranged a number of events. And one of the options on offer was a visit to the Auschwitz camp, which I must say was really quite overwhelming.

The archives reveal the role that the American representative, Jack Maresca, played at the CSCE in 1990: Did you notice it?

I have known Maresca, but after the Paris Summit. I took part in numerous meetings of the Committee of Senior Officials, which had been established by the Charter of Paris. And Maresca was my American counterpart.

Maresca and I, all too often, would end up sparring over the question of NATO. This entailed going through the documents, screeds and screeds of text, in order to prepare for the conference. Each of us had his own version and so sometimes I would see passages in Maresca's American version that I disagreed with (they were usually formulations concerning NATO). I would say: "Forgive me, but I am going to have to put brackets around this passage." To which Maresca would retort: "I see, very well then, I shall just have to put brackets around that other passage in your document." We spent our time bracketing each other's texts! More often than not, there would be some neutral party – or sometimes a representative from the UK – who would timidly speak up and suggest: "We might be able to reach a compromise." At that time, I had my two deputies, Pierre Filatoff[15] and Roland Galharague,[16] with me and I would say to one or to the other: "Quick, call Paris immediately, and ask them if we can accept this wording." The answer would generally be: "Yes, they are fine with that." That was how things worked, and the

---

[14] Franciszek Macharski: Polish Cardinal, Archbishop of Krakow from 1978 to 2005.

[15] Pierre Filatoff: French diplomat, serving at the Europe Directorate (1990-1993) and later at the Strategic Affairs, Security and Disarmament Directorate (1993-1997).

[16] Roland Galharague: French diplomat, Europe Directorate (1990-1993).

TESTIMONIALS

Speech by Mr Dumas before the CSCE in Helsinki, July 1992.

> The Helsinki Summit marks a step towards the institutionalisation of the CSCE, with the creation of the High Commissioner on National Minorities and the establishment of security cooperation actions.

atmosphere was relatively cordial. The same cannot be said for the American representative in Helsinki in 1992 – it was not Maresca – whose proposal I managed to block in the Heads of State plenary; it would have paved the way for NATO interventions to be placed on a par with those of the United Nations.

ILLUSTRATION BOOK

Arrival of François Mitterrand to the European Council in Strasbourg, 8-9 December 1989.

President-in-Office of the European Community, François Mitterrand takes a firm stand for German reunification to take place within the framework of European integration.

ILLUSTRATION BOOK

Arrival of Felipe Gonzalez and Helmut Kohl to the European Council in Strasbourg, 8-9 December 1989.

Eagerly awaited by his European partners due to his positions on European integration, Federal Chancellor Kohl would later say that he had "never experienced such an icy atmosphere during a European summit".

ILLUSTRATION BOOK

Arrival of Margaret Thatcher and Douglas Hurd
to the European Council meeting in Strasbourg, 8-9 December 1989.

Reputed for being hostile to reunification, Margaret Thatcher pressures Germany and demands that it comply with the positions of its European partners.

Official visit to France by General Jaruzelski, President of the Republic of Poland, and Prime Minister Tadeusz Mazowiecki, 9 March 1990.

After Roland Dumas criticized on 1 March in Berlin Germany's "loud silence of ambiguity" on the establishment of the border with Poland, the President and the Prime Minister of Poland went to Paris to re-apply pressure on Federal Chancellor Kohl. The question of the German-Polish border was finally settled by the Treaty of Moscow and the German-Polish Treaty of 14 November 1990, via which Germany renounced all territorial demands in Poland.

ILLUSTRATION BOOK

Vaclav Havel and François Mitterrand at the first official visit to France by a President of the Republic of Czechoslovakia, 19-21 March 1990.

Long opposing the Communist regime, the most prominent leader of the Velvet Revolution, Vaclav Havel, is received at the Elysée Palace by François Mitterrand, just after he was elected President of Czechoslovakia.

ILLUSTRATION BOOK

Signature by Pierre Bérégovoy, François Mitterrand and Roland Dumas
of the Agreement establishing the European Bank
for Reconstruction and Development (EBRD), Elysée, 29 May 1990.

The EBRD, proposed by Jacques Attali, marks Europeans' commitment to the economic development of Eastern Europe.

Signature of the Treaty on the Final Settlement with Respect to Germany in Moscow on 12 September 1990. *From left to right:* James Baker, Douglas Hurd, Edouard Chevardnadze, Roland Dumas, Lothar de Maizière, and Hans-Dietrich Genscher.

The Treaty of Moscow (or 2+4 Treaty) was signed by the four powers which occupied Germany in 1945 and by the representatives of East Germany and West Germany.

ILLUSTRATION BOOK

Visit to Weimar, German Democratic Republic (GDR), by Roland Dumas and Hans-Dietrich Genscher, after the signature of the Treaty of Moscow, September 1990.

This private visit by the two ministers to the GDR testifies to their special understanding and shows France's support for the reunification process.

ILLUSTRATION BOOK

Roland Dumas and Hans-Dietrich Genscher travelling by helicopter from Halle to Weimar (GDR), September 1990.

ILLUSTRATION BOOK

Roland Dumas, Edouard Chevardnadze, Douglas Hurd, Hans-Dietrich Genscher and James A. Baker celebrate their good relations on the sidelines of the Meeting of Foreign Ministers of CSCE Participating States in New York, October 1990.

ILLUSTRATION BOOK

Overview of the hall during Roland Dumas' speech
at the Meeting of Foreign Ministers of CSCE Participating States in New York,
October 1990.

ILLUSTRATION BOOK

Robert Badinter and Roland Dumas at a luncheon of prominent figures organized before the Paris Summit, 10 November 1990.

With a view to the CSCE Summit of 19 to 21 November, Roland Dumas brings together prominent members of civil society at the Foreign Ministry to discuss the future of Europe.

ILLUSTRATION BOOK

Portrait of Margaret Thatcher
in the conference room
at the Ministry of Foreign Affairs,
avenue Kléber, 19 November 1990.

Portrait of Mikhail Gorbachev
at the Paris Summit, November 1990.

ILLUSTRATION BOOK

Portraits of Mikhail Gorbachev in the Conference Room
of the Ministry of Foreign Affairs, avenue Kléber, 19 November 1990.

Meeting between
George H. W. Bush
and Mikhail Gorbachev
at the Paris Summit,
November 1990.

Portraits of George H. W. Bush in the Conference Room
of the Ministry of Foreign Affairs, avenue Kléber, 19 November 1990.

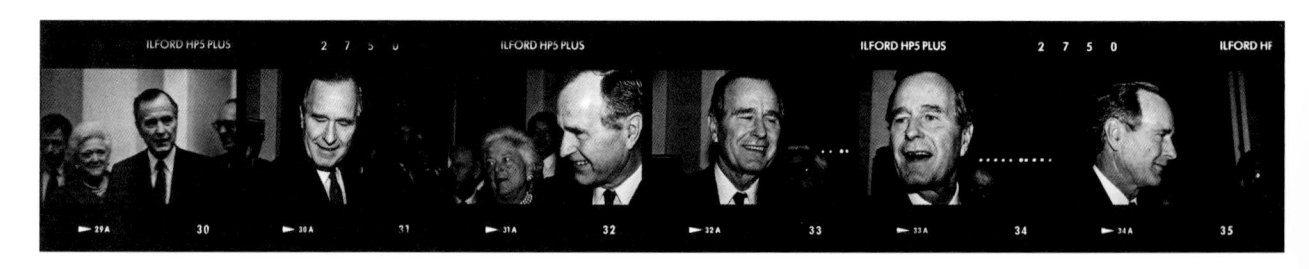

ILLUSTRATION BOOK

Press Conference given by Helmut Kohl
at the Paris Summit, November 1990.

Portraits of Helmut Kohl
in the Conference Room
of the Ministry of Foreign Affairs,
avenue Kléber, 19 November 1990.

ILLUSTRATION BOOK

AV664 Audiovisual Fund.

François Mitterrand at the signing of the Treaty on Conventional Forces in Europe (CFE) at the Elysée Palace, on 19 November 1990.

AV664 Audiovisual Fund.

Arrival of the Heads of State and Government at the International Conference Centre on avenue Kléber, on 19 November 1990.

UNPUBLISHED ARCHIVES
OF THE PREPARATORY COMMITTEE NEGOTIATIONS IN VIENNA

Meeting of Foreign Ministers of the CSCE Member States in New York,
1st-2nd November 1990.

Requested by the United States. The New York meeting, the first CSCE meeting in the United States, marks their commitment to the CSCE process.

UNPUBLISHED ARCHIVES OF THE PREPARATORY COMMITTEE NEGOTIATIONS IN VIENNA

1

Mr Morel, Head of the French delegation (Proper address?)
    To the central administration

Diplomatic Telegram Vienna 417   **11 July 1990.**

Conference on Security and Co-operation in Europe (CSCE). Preparatory Committee for the Paris Summit – Opening of proceedings (1/2)

> Summary:
>
> Albania: Observer State.

The Preparatory Committee for the Paris Summit of the Conference on Security and Co-operation in Europe opened on 10 July with an address by Mr Thomas Klestil, Secretary General of the Austrian Ministry of Foreign Affairs.

Mr Klestil and the other speakers emphasized the historic importance of the Paris Summit, called upon to make fundamental decisions on the future of Europe and to lay down guidance in all the CSCE's fields. He also considered that Paris would mark both a culmination and a starting point of a new phase of the Helsinki process. He highlighted the importance of the Preparatory Committee's task.

At the opening of the plenary session, the Austrian President informed the 35 participating states of the Albanian Government's wish to attend the proceedings of the Committee as an observer, following the precedent set in Copenhagen. I am reporting to the Central administration in a separate Diplomatic Telegram on the prior consultations that took place on this issue, which revealed the absence of any procedural rules to object to the presence of the Albanian delegation.

The representative of Italy made two statements on behalf of the Twelve. The first statement on Albania, which repeated the terms agreed by the 12 member States on the matter, had been previously communicated to the Central Administration (see my Diplomatic Telegram No 410). The second was of a general nature and dealt with the Summit action lines on the basis of the conclusions adopted by the Dublin European Council.

The head of the US delegation, Mr Maresca, focused on the importance of the London Declaration on a transformed North Atlantic Alliance, and especially on the need to actively prepare for the ministerial meeting of the 35 in New York. He proposed 1 and 2 October and stated that he would like to receive a response from the respective governments by 17 July in order to begin preparations.

The representative of Poland, Mr Konarski, reminded those present of the initiative taken by his country, the GDR and Czechoslovakia to set up mechanisms for political consultations and institutional bodies which, in his view, were indispensable in the area of security.

He noted that the Paris Summit could welcome the first anniversary of the profound changes that had taken place in Europe, but that it should above all serve to guarantee and protect the "still fragile democracies" that were emerging. Finally, Mr Konarski welcomed the content of the Declaration on a transformed North Atlantic Alliance.

The head of the Austrian delegation, Mr Vukovich, gave a lengthy speech describing the possible content of the Summit's concluding document. In his opinion, it should cover: 1) the strengthening of the Helsinki Decalogue through commitments relating to the rule of law and democratic institutions agreed in Copenhagen. All of these commitments should now be of a legal nature; 2) the signature of the Treaty on Conventional Armed Forces in Europe (CFE) and the adoption of a document on Confidence and Security Building Measures (CSBMs), the decision to continue negotiations on security with the objective of achieving a single mandate from the 35 participating States at Helsinki II in 1992; 3) the development of Basket II, justified by the need for economic assistance from the Eastern countries; 4) under the framework of the "Human Dimension", the rights of national minorities and the decision to convene a meeting of experts in Switzerland in this regard; 5) the strengthening of the Human Rights Council (HRC) mechanism and various institutional arrangements – mechanisms for consultations at different levels, a permanent secretariat and the creation of a military security agency responsible for verification.

The Austrian delegate also stressed the role that could be played by the "Pentagonale" countries and pointed out that the European process should continue to include both the Soviet Union and the North American countries.

The head of the German delegation, Mr zu Rantzau, delivered the speech he had referred to earlier (see Diplomatic Telegram Bonn 1806), which focused on the content of the concluding document. The document should be concise, substantial and solemn. It should be a single document with technical annexes to preserve the highly political nature of the text.

The document could be in three parts: 1) affirmation of the CSCE *acquis*, its contribution to developments and its role in the future architecture of Europe on the basis of the rule of law, human rights, protection of minorities, etc. ; 2) strengthening of security and cooperation in Europe (CAF and CSBMs) and the follow-up to these negotiations. Orientations for a democratic Europe and for the future of economic cooperation (in principle, the German question is taken into account here, but Mr zu Rantzau omitted this point in his speech, considering that it was not for him to refer to it); 3) decisions of an institutional nature, political consultation mechanism, conflict prevention centre, participation of parliamentary assemblies, link with the Council of Europe.

The head of the Soviet delegation, Mr Deryabin, underscored the historic importance of the Paris Summit. He stressed that the Bonn and Copenhagen meetings had each made significant progress in their respective areas. It was now important to take disarmament to that level. An "ideas bank" for collective or individual suggestions was available for this purpose. The Soviet delegate cited Mr Shevardnadze's letter, the June declarations by the Warsaw Pact members, as well as documents from Dublin (12) and London (16). (To be continued)./.

Mr Morel, Head of the French delegation
  To the central administration

Diplomatic Telegram Vienna 418   11 July 1990.

Opening of the Preparatory Committee for the CSCE Summit in Paris: preliminary findings (1/2)

> Summary:
>
> Position of the Twelve and non-aligned countries; ambitions of Maresca, Head of the US delegation.

The first day of preparations leading up to the CSCE Summit in Paris next November leaves a somewhat mixed impression. Many delegations are uncomfortable with the Preparatory Committee, which are currently trying to find theirbearings. But the key players have been clear from day one, and the debate on the role and nature of this unprecedented Summit has already begun.

1. Behind the customary politeness and good humour inherent in any meeting of the Helsinki family, one can sense in many delegations – especially small and medium ones – a certain disarray in the face of an event that they have not yet fully grasped and which goes against the weight of custom, rule of procedure and religion of the previous one. Those who no longer fully recognize "their" CSCE may take some time to find their bearings. They have participated in endless consultations within the groups on organizational matters, but they refrained from speaking in plenary sessions, with the result that only nine delegations spoke onthe opening day, occupying only half of the time available.

We should also note the composite nature of the delegations, led for some countries by the representative who was present at the 35-party negotiations on confidence-building measures, who then wished to adapt the Committee's work to the weekly constraints of the negotiations under the Vienna mandate.

This widespread inertia inevitably affects the work of the groups. The Twelve remain rather hesitant for the moment, as they have not yet moved beyond the general guidelines stage. For its part, the United States delegation has sought to demonstrate to the Western Group that it would find the answer to all its questions by engaging in a methodical preparation by the Sixteen of all the elements of the outcome document. But there is so much support for this operation that it should lead the countries of the community topull themselves together, and other allies to distance themselves from what does not suit them.

As for the non-aligned countries, which have been very quiet up to now, they (judging from the new Poland and Czechoslovakia) can see that the good days of quasi-obligatory mediation between East and West will not return. The first reflex, judging by Austria, even if the concerns of the Committee's host country have to be taken into account, was to seek to consolidate past achievements, hence the idea, proposed by the head of the delegation in his contribution, of giving legal force to the ten principles of the Final Act, and the extensive inventory of the three baskets, seeking each time to identify the most appropriate institutional extension. But at the same time Vienna was thinking of other means of action; Mr Vukovich did not speak at any time about the neutral and non-aligned countries (N+N), but referred to the "Pentagonale" countries. As for Finland, it is already focusing its attention on what is most important to it, namely the preparation of the Helsinki meeting in 1992, the groundwork for which should be laid at the Paris Summit.

2. The fact remains that the the game was on from day one. The head of the US delegation is determined to take the lead at all times, be it in his speech, among the first speakers, at the opening session (see separate telegram), at Western meetings, or intalks. The attempt to take control of the Western "caucus" is no surprise considering the personal commitment of Mr Maresca, author of a book on the CSCE, and can be explained by his perception of the American turnaround as a "divine surprise": the display of a very dynamic approach is finally de rigueur after the London Summit. However, it should be noted that there is a willingness to immediately start to prepare the building blocks for the Final Act and, even more so, the disproportionate place that the US representative is giving to the ministerial meeting of the 35 in New York on 1 and 2 October next.

This last point merits special attention. During the Western meeting preceding the opening, the US representative stressed that this was the "first official CSCE event on US soil", it would certainly attract media attention, and should be carefully prepared. This statement immediately provoked very strong reactions from the German, British and Dutch delegations, and of course from ourselves. After giving a reply which sought to reassure us of the pre-eminence of the Paris Summit, a little later in his contribution, Mr Maresca nevertheless proposed to the plenary that the preparation of the Committee should be one of the three items on the Committee's agenda by the end of July. A subsequent exchange of views with the Italians and the Germans suggests that the Twelve will come back very firmly on this subject. I note that Mr Maresca proposes to organize next Friday, in the discreet form of a lunch, a four-party meeting to take stock of the Committee's launch: this will be an opportunity for an even more direct warning.

In his statement, the gist of which had been communicated the day before to the Twelve (my fax No 2), the FRG representative, Mr zu Rantzau, was the first to propose a detailed outline for the final document of the Paris Summit: a single text with a preamble and three main parts, noting the changes, reaffirming the principles and strengthening the role of the CSCE, guidelines for the main chapters, and institutional aspects. I note that the reference to the German question, curiously placed at the end of Part Two in the text submitted to the Twelve ("acknowledgement of the results achieved in the negotiations on German unification, in particular its final settlement under international law") was, according to its author, "the result of a regrettable error", and was not repeated in his public speech. This ambitious framework will give us something to work on with the Germans because it is too rigid and repetitive. As for the idea of a single text, my German colleague has already told me that he did not want to impede us on this point. (To be continued). Signed: P. Morel./.

Mr Morel, Head of the French delegation
   To the central administration

Diplomatic Telegram Vienna 419   **11 July 1990.**

Conference on Security and Co-operation in Europe (CSCE). Preparatory Committee for the Paris Summit – Opening of proceedings (2/2)

> Summary:
>
> Czechoslovakia, Finland: institutionalization of the CSCE.

The head of the Czechoslovak delegation spoke (in Russian) quite firmly. He indicated that the first objective of the Summit should be the registration of the CFE and CSBM agreements. It should also welcome the "end of dictatorships". Finally, he recalled the importance attached by his country to a form of institutionalization of the CSCE, in particular the trilateral proposal with the GDR and Poland. Finally, he hoped that the Committee would be able to propose a first set of recommendations to Ministers at their meeting in New York.

The head of the Finnish delegation, Mr Reimaa, recalled Finland's long-standing specific interest in the CSCE process and its then premature proposal in Madrid for a Standing Committee. He expressed his satisfaction to see that times had changed. He stressed that Europe's "functional needs" should be the basis for proposals on institutionalization. The adaptability and flexibility of the CSCE should be maintained, as well as the principle of sovereign equality of member States. Finland would support the idea of periodic meetings of Heads of State and Government and Foreign Ministers. The Paris Summit should provide action lines for the Helsinki meeting in 1992.

At the end of the first day's discussions, it was decided to adopt a provisional programme of work consisting exclusively of daily plenary meetings until the end of the week. Informal discussions should make it possible to agree, by the end of the session, on a working method better suited to the nature of the negotiations. (GF/RG). Signed: P. Morel./.

4

Mr Morel, Head of the French delegation
    To the central administration

Diplomatic Telegram Vienna 420   11 July 1990.

Opening of the Preparatory Committee for the CSCE Summit in Paris: preliminary findings (2/2)

> Summary:
>
> Soviet insistence on a security architecture; French declaration in favour of "a democratic, peaceful and united Europe, the development of security and cooperation, and institutional arrangements"; declaration of non-aggression.

On the USSR, it should be noted that Mr Deryabin's speech did not contain many concrete elements: the Soviet Union had a duty to speak on the first day, but is waiting to make a public statement.

My first meeting with Mr Deryabin was more enlightening: he wants to set a "substantial agenda" for the Summit instead of the "insignificant programme" which, according to him, some would like to settle for (opening, speeches, adoption of the document(s)). In fact, he is seeking an initial agreement on the essential points followed by the definition of the document outline, and then tackling, in his own words, "the question of possible institutions" on the basis of the already extensive inventory of proposals. It should be noted that he is very cautious on this last point, which led him to urge that institutionalization should not be an end in itself but a means.

As for the idea of a declaration of non-aggression adopted at the Summit, Mr Deryabin initially described the idea yesterday as "interesting and impressive". His deputy added that the Paris Summit should mark the beginning of a gradual transition towards a collective security system in order to respond to the opponents of Gorbachev's policies. However, the Soviet representative appears to have later indicated to the Germans that the preliminary step of a joint declaration by the Alliance and the Pact was an essential precondition for acceptance of united Germany's membership of NATO. The two-stage format of the Alliance's declaration would therefore be preferred. The question is worth taking up directly with Mr Deryabin, who referred insistently to the Franco-Soviet tradition linked to the CSCE to mark his readiness to cooperate with us in the run-up to the Summit.

Finally, we must consider the speeches of Poland and Czechoslovakia because they demonstrate, with some precautions here and there, the internal transformation of these countries (there was something strange about Mr Balcar referring in Russian to the "end of dictatorship") and outline the attitude of the new democracies of central Europe: balanced references to the London Declaration and Mr Shevardnadze's proposals, insistence on the tripartite proposal, with the GDR, of a Council for Security and Cooperation in Europe as a means of speeding up the exit from the blocs, and lastly and above all the search for collective and multidimensional European support to deal with internal difficulties.

In this kick-off of the first day, we had to do our bit: I note that after our speech (see separate telegram), various delegations expressed their interest in our reminder of the specific nature of the Paris Summit, which is very different to the Helsinki Summit, in our recommendations for a step-by-step preparation, and in the grouping of subjects under three clearly identified themes: democratic, peaceful and united Europe, development of security and cooperation, and institutional arrangements.

We now need to move on to the next step and prepare working papers quickly, and in the appropriate format.

Together with the Twelve, we should tackle the "Declaration on a Democratic Europe", which will undoubtedly be a laborious task, but, considering the outcome of the Dublin Summit, it is in our interest to involve our partners in this very important text, which sets out the general direction we want to give to the Paris Summit.

With the Sixteen, one can expect the systematic exploitation, with draft texts in support, of the relevant paragraphs of the London Declaration. Perhaps we could counter this offensive by submitting our own working paper on the most sensitive point, namely the nature, functions and title of the centre for risk (or conflict) prevention and transparency. In addition, we must prepare for difficult discussions, after the ongoing consultation of the governments on our vision of a declaration of non-aggression to be signed in Paris by the 35: the Belgians and the Spanish are sensitive to our arguments on the futility of a revival of the Warsaw Pact, on the disadvantage of placing the NNAs[1] in second place, and on the central nature of such a document according to the ten principles. But the British argue that the two-stage initiative launched by the Heads of State and Government in London cannot be altered in Vienna. As for the Germans, they will agree with the Soviets.

I would be grateful for the Central Administration's feedback on these points. Signed: P. Morel./.

---

[1] Neutral and non-aligned countries.

5

Mr Morel, Head of the French delegation
  To the central administration

Diplomatic Telegram Vienna 478   23 July 1990.

Conference on Security and Co-operation in Europe (CSCE). Preparatory Committee for the Paris Summit. Day of 20 July. (1/2)

> Summary:
>
> Minorities, security and disarmament, economic issues.

The last day of the week was marked by several national contributions on the content of the Summit document. These should enable the coordinator of the *ad hoc* group to draw up an initial inventory of the elements under discussion and a draft working structure by Monday. In the official plenary session, I gave a speech outlining our view of the first part of the declaration (see separate Diplomatic Telegram) and announced the submission of a non-paper specifying the detailed outline. At the *ad hoc* group meeting that followed, this non-paper was introduced along with other drafts from the US delegation, the Canadian delegation and the Norwegian delegation. I also report on the restricted consultations that took place on the same day (see my Diplomatic Telegram No 477), during which issues relating to the Summit's agenda and the organization of work in September were discussed. Finally, the dates for the end of the session, on 27 July, and for the resumption of work, on 4 September, were formally adopted.

1/ At the plenary session, following my speech, the text of which was sent to the Central Administration by fax No 12, the Finnish and then the US representative took the floor. The Finnish representative welcomed the activities of the *ad hoc* group and hoped that this first session would confirm the agreement in principle of the 35 on a list of elements to be included in the Summit document, to specify its agenda, and to establish the working structure of the Committee. In this respect, he recalled the value of the traditional methods of the CSCE, and in particular the benefits of having coordinators.

The representative of the US delegation took the floor to comment briefly on my speech. After a few positive remarks on our general approach, he wished to immediately raise two points which presented difficulties for his delegation: the declaration of non-aggression – an initiative which, in his view, belonged to the members of the alliances – and the transition to a single 35-party negotiation on disarmament, an issue which had not yet been discussed and which the US authorities, like other Western countries, considered premature, preferring the current dual-track negotiating format.

2/ The meeting of the *ad hoc* group allowed several delegations, including our own, to distribute non-papers outlining their ideas on the content of the Summit document. Each delegation stressed that these were contributions to the discussion and were not intended to replace the documents already submitted by the Twelve and the NNAs, but could serve as supplements.

...

The Austrian coordinator, Mr Lehne, indicated that he would prepare, in principle by Monday, a list identifying the common, or complementary, non-controversial elements of the documents available to him at this stage. From the full exchange of views, once again during this meeting, the following points were made: on minorities – Switzerland, Austria and Hungary asked for explicit reference to a meeting of experts to be convened by the Summit. The US representative, the Romanian representative and a few others expressed some reservations on this point, as the initiative appears somewhat premature to them. A debate was then held on the feasibility of such a meeting as early as 1991, either before the next stage of the Conference on the Human Dimension in Moscow, or by Helsinki II, or even at a later date. Our representative pointed out that, at this stage, the task of the *ad hoc* group was to identify elements and concepts to facilitate the transition to the drafting phase and not to take formal decisions, in particular on convening new meetings of experts.

That said, in Copenhagen the 35 had already expressed interest in the principle of a meeting on minorities, therefore the Committee could consider that matter in due course, i.e. when the content of the document has been defined and decisions taken on a possible follow-up to the Summit.

On security, the neutrals intervened to emphasize the need to reflect on the transition to a 35-party negotiation on disarmament, which could take place after Helsinki II in 1992. The US and Dutch representatives recalled that, in their view, the issue was premature and that only the two negotiations – with the 23 and the 35 participating states – should be continued.

Several delegations also requested that the issue of counter-terrorism be added to the security agenda.

On economic cooperation and the environment, the idea of assistance for "emerging democracies" was supported by many delegations, as was the mention of social justice. The Czechoslovak representative suggested that a meeting on the subject of economies in transition should be organized in 1991 with the contribution of the OECD and the UNECE. Finally, on the environment, the Norwegian suggestions were well received, apart from the reference to a "code of conduct". On the other hand, the Austrian representative suggested introducing the concept of a "social and ecological market economy" as a model for the future Europe.

On culture, it was agreed to add the idea of diversity to that of community in the text of the Twelve, and to specify the training commitments to be made.

On the Mediterranean, the Spanish representative stressed that the Palma meeting was tasked with addressing cooperation, particularly on environmental issues, while security issues, if they needed to be raised, were the responsibility of the Preparatory Committee. (To be continued). (GF). Signed: P. Morel./.

6

**Letter from Mr James A. Baker, Secretary of State of the United States of America
To Mr Roland Dumas, French Minister of Foreign Affairs**

21 September 1990.

> Summary:
>
> United States' insistence on the conclusion of the Treaty on Conventional Armed Forces at the Paris Summit.

Dear Roland:

The successful completion of the two-plus-four process brings to a close another chapter of postwar history. With German unification and a unified Germany's place in NATO secure, we need to focus our attention on issues that must be resolved if we are to complete the foundation for the new European architecture: concluding the CFE agreement and, on that basis, moving ahead with the CSCE summit.

All of us have agreed at NATO that a completed CFE agreement is an essential part of the CSCE summit. Foreign minister Shevardnadze has exactly the same view. In Moscow last week, I made clear that he and the rest of the Soviet political leadership will have to turn their attention more directly to CFE if we are to resolve the major issues still outstanding, so that our negotiators in Vienna can then come to closure on the details of an agreement.

With the CSCE ministerial in New York approaching, I want to review with you where I think we stand on CFE and give you our views on what additional elements of a CFE treaty must be agreed for us to complete the CFE treaty and move ahead with the CSCE summit.

Effective verification of a CFE accord is crucial to our common security, and is thus a sine qua non of treaty signature and ratification. In that light, it is essential to resolve favourably the differences between Soviet and NATO approaches to on-site inspection.

Similarly, Soviet-proposed sub-limits on ground equipment in the central zone would squeeze Eastern European militaries below the levels that they deem necessary for their national defence, and halve NATO forces there. This also is simply out of the question. Nor does the Soviet idea of dropping the central zone or deferring the zones to follow-on negotiations seem to me to offer any promise of resolving this issue in a way that would allow us to complete the CFE treaty this year. At the same time, I think we should be prepared to tell the Soviets that we are willing to address the issue of zones further in the follow-on negotiations.

On the sufficiency rule, as with central zone limits, the relative military strength of the Soviet Union in Europe is at stake – a fundamental underpinning of future arms control talks and of the soviet role in European affairs. The West is not alone in rejecting the Soviet idea of a sufficiency rule of "at least forty percent" – the Eastern Europeans do so as well. However, in order to come to closure on this issue, we should be prepared to offer a sufficiency rule higher than thirty per cent – e.g., an average of thirty-three and a third per cent, as proposed by the Hungarians, with the possibility of a higher sufficiency rule for aircraft.

We are willing to take the Soviet concerns into account on the conversion issue. We have come a long way in reaching agreement with the east on modalities for destruction and conversion. The Soviet demand for the right to convert, rather than destroy, up to 9,000 armoured vehicles is much too high. That said, if conversion procedures that effectively eliminate military capability can be agreed, we should be prepared to accept a number significantly higher than the current NATO position.

A fifth question is aircraft. The initiative advanced by our Heads of State and Government in May 1989 provided a bold and equitable approach to this important problem – an approach which we have been willing to modify in an equitable fashion if our flexibility is reciprocated. But the Soviet Union – most recently in our sessions last week in Moscow – continues to show no sign of wishing to reach a balanced outcome on aircraft. If we want this negotiation to limit aircraft in a satisfactory way, I believe we must insist that any limits in or associated with the CFE treaty must numerically constrain land-based naval aircraft. These limits should not allow each side a total beyond the 6,000s, and not entitle the Soviet Union alone to a total of more than about 5,000. If such limits, and particularly LBNA limits, cannot be achieved, then in our view we should postpone the treatment of aircraft to the follow-on negotiations.

As allies, we must all seek every opportunity to press our concerns aggressively in our bilateral contacts with the Soviets over the coming weeks, to supplement our collective efforts in Vienna. I intend to do this with Shevardnadze in my meetings with him on 26 September. Furthermore, I am convinced of the effectiveness of our linkage between a completed CFE agreement and the holding of a CSCE summit. I will reemphasize with Shevardnadze that unless these issues are rapidly resolved, we cannot get there. As we have consistently said, the United States will not attend a CSCE summit without a completed CFE agreement.

I would appreciate hearing your views on these important questions as soon as possible and look forward to our meetings in New York.

Sincerely,

/S/

James A. Baker, III

His Excellency
    Roland Dumas
        Ministre d'État
            Minister of Foreign Affairs
            75007 Paris

7

Mr Morel, Head of the French delegation
   To the central administration

Diplomatic Telegram Vienna 854   **19 October 1990.**

CSCE – Preparatory Committee for the Paris Summit. Ministre d'État's talks with Mr Shevardnadze in Vienna (18 October)

> Summary:
>
> Harmonization of the French and Soviet positions on disarmament and institutionalization of the CSCE.

As with the CAF negotiations, the two ministers considered that the good cooperation between France and the USSR in Vienna should make it possible, as deadlines were approaching, to act together to reach out to other countries.

1/ On the first part of the document, the Soviet delegation insisted on the importance it attached to the declaration of the 22 members of the alliances, which would be signed by the Heads of State and Government. Mr Shevardnadze enquired as to the reasons for the US delegation's reserve on the text by the 34, and Mr Deryabin referred to Washington's fears that the ten Helsinki principles might be modified, adding that this was obviously not the case, it was merely to highlight the most relevant ones in light of the changes that had taken place. For our part, we recalled the importance of the Franco-Soviet agreement in principle reached between the two ministers on 26 August in Moscow on a balanced treatment of the two texts of the 22 and 34 participating States.

2/ On the question of the mandate for future disarmament negotiations by the 35, Mr Shevardnadze likewise enquired about the United States' attitude, but did not give any indication of the Soviet position. The Ministre d'État noted that the impatience of the non-aligned countries to start negotiations on the mandate immediately after the Paris Summit overlooked the real issue, namely the details that should be addressed in this new framework from 1992 onwards. A lot would happen in Europe between now and then: rather than fighting for the mandate, we had to think actively about it.

3/ On institutional arrangements, the Soviet representative noted that, since an agreement in principle had been reached among the delegations, much remained to be done to clarify the functions and terms of reference of the various bodies to be established. Mr Deryabin recalled the Soviet view that the conflict prevention centre would initially have military functions, but could later develop its capabilities in the area of political conflicts. With regard to the CSCE Parliamentary Assembly, the two Ministers noted the US turnaround on the method of its establishment and the relationship with the Council of Europe.

At the end of the meeting, Mr Shevardnadze expressed his concern about the challenges that needed to be addressed between now and the Paris Summit, particularly with regard to the CAFs, which risked remaining open until the meeting itself. Some last-minute technical issues could become insurmountable due to lack of time to clarify them. It was to be expected that one or more of the participating States might play up. The Ministre d'État concluded that this was an additional reason to act together to reach out to other delegations. Signed: P. Morel./.

Noiville

8

Disarmament Department
    at the central administration

Diplomatic Telegram Vienna 879   **19 October 1990.**

Ministre d'État's talks with Mr Shevardnadze in Vienna (18 October) CAF

> Summary:
>
> Disarmament: the case of Turkey and strategic bombers.

On the subject of the negotiation on Conventional Armed Forces, the two Ministers considered that we should combine our efforts to overcome the remaining challenges and thus have a knock-on effect on other delegations.

1) After underscoring that the bilateral consultations followed by the compromise reached in New York had made it possible to speed up negotiations, both Mr Shevardnadze and Mr Grinevsky complained about the attitude of Turkey, which was threatening not to sign the treaty. The positions agreed with Mr Baker constituted a comprehensive, balanced package. The special treatment of paramilitary forces equipment was an element of this. If Turkey reneged on the New York compromise and demanded that paramilitary equipment be treated in the same way as that of Conventional Armed Forces, the treaty might not be signed on 19 November. Political pressure should therefore be exerted on Turkey for it not to call into question the agreement reached. Mr Grinevsky suggested reaching out to Ankara.

2) The Political importance of the sufficiency rule of one third was stressed by the French.

3) The Ministre d'État recalled that we were considering a unilateral declaration repeating the reservation made by the President of the Republic in Brussels on our strategic bombers. If this solution was acceptable to all participants, it needed to be taken forward. We had discussed this with the Soviet delegation and were awaiting their response.

For Mr Shevardnadze, the USSR could not agree to put its strategic bombers on the table at the Vienna negotiations since they would be covered by the START agreement. The idea of a unilateral declaration by France was interesting. It could, for example, be done at the time of signing the treaty in Paris. It was agreed that the heads of delegation would continue the discussion on this point in Vienna.

4) For the Ministre d'État, the question of Alphajet aircraft should be settled according to their level of armament. We invited interested delegations to come to Tours next week for a presentation of these aircraft. Anyone would be able to see immediately that these types

of aircraft were used for basic training only and could not be considered fighter aircraft. The German case was different.

Mr Shevardnadze announced that the Soviet delegation would be represented in Tours. The issue of Alphajet seemed to him to be a technical problem that could be "resolved in a satisfactory manner".

5) Transfers east of the Urals

According to the Soviet Minister, the necessary clarifications had already been given, in particular during the Ministre d'État's visit to Moscow. Additional information would be provided, as necessary, at the time of the ratification debate.

The Ministre d'État pointed out that the world had hitherto lived in mistrust, which had led to the arms race. Disarmament should therefore be based, *mutatis mutandis*, on trust and not on mistrust. The fundamental issue which had to be settled was still that of trust.

Why would the Soviet Union not organise a visit of the armaments transferred beyond the Urals ? That would be the best way to answer the concerns./.

Poudade

9

Mr Morel, Head of the French delegation
    To the central administration

Diplomatic Telegram Vienna 945   *7 November 1990.*

CSCE – Preparatory Committee for the Paris Summit. Lunch with the Four

> Summary:
>
> Position of the Four (France, United Kingdom, United States, Germany): case of Yugoslavia, preparation of the agenda for the informal debate planned during the Paris Summit.

During the weekly lunch of the Four, the discussion focused on the situation in Yugoslavia, which the US delegation wishes to raise at the Summit, the agenda for the informal debate between Heads of State or Government, and the question of the Assembly of Europe.

1) The Head of the US delegation spoke about the current thinking in Washington regarding the possibility of addressing the situation in Yugoslavia during the Summit. Speaking off the record in a personal capacity, Mr Maresca said that the idea of a "declaration" on the subject seemed unrealistic, but in order to convince his superiors, something else had to be proposed: for example, he thought that, along with the US delegation, several allies could address the issue in their speeches at the Summit or even at press conferences.

The reaction of my British and German colleagues was negative. A declaration by the 34 on this subject was of course inconceivable, and any explicit reference to Yugoslavia in an official speech seemed to them to be out of the question, since it was not clear how publicly undermining the Yugoslav government could improve such a complex and delicate situation. For my part, I recalled the discussion that took place in Evere and recommended that we take a positive approach by stressing in the speeches and in the document the need to strengthen stability and overcome divisions in Europe.

2) A first exchange of views took place on the possible agenda for the informal debate on Tuesday, 20 November. I reminded my colleagues that, based on initial opinion-gathering, three topics had emerged: the Gulf crisis, the difficulties of economic transition, and the question of minorities. Furthermore, in order to be able to discuss difficult topics such as Cyprus without naming them, some countries like Greece were considering a more general point, such as a "review of the situation in Europe", which could serve either as an introductory or concluding discussion. My colleagues agreed that there was indeed a need for a convenient way to in principle allow everyone to express themselves, while avoiding laborious negotiations in Vienna or Paris on the inclusion of controversial items in the agenda of the informal debate.

3) The question of the Assembly of Europe was only briefly discussed. Mr Maresca announced Mr Spencer Oliver's forthcoming visit to Vienna and suggested that we should seek compromise formulas with him. My German and British colleagues and I rejected any idea of direct negotiations with the congressman. If he asked to meet with us, we could remind him of our positions and of the need to give effect, in a manner acceptable to all, to the commitment made by the Heads of State and Government in the Alliance's London Declaration. For the rest, the task of convincing congressional representatives fell to the US delegation. For our part, of course, we remained ready to seek compromise formulas. (GF) Signed: P. Morel./.

Noiville

10

Mr Morel, Head of the French delegation
    To the central administration
Diplomatic Telegram Vienna 946   7 November 1990.

CSCE – Preparatory Committee for the Paris Summit. Organization of the Summit

> Summary:
>
> Position of the Four (France, United Kingdom, United States, Germany): status of Albania and the Baltic States, organization of the Paris Summit.

The meeting of the informal group of "friends of the Paris Summit" on 5 November and contacts on the sidelines of this meeting discussed the following points:

1. Status of Albania

We proposed the adoption of a special paragraph in the "organizational framework" providing for observer status (see my telegram No 926). This text was not adopted because of reservations, pending answers to a request for instructions, by the Turkish and US delegations. It will be reviewed and most likely adopted on Friday, 9 November.

2. Baltic States

The delegations are still waiting for us to tell them which Baltic representatives are invited to the Summit. I would like to point out that if the Baltic States can be admitted to observe, this will not be enough to satisfy the concerns of the delegations. It is also essential for formal invitations to be issued within the host country's contingent (which has the advantage of being the most "neutral" formula for the 34, as the host country can be considered to some extent as representing all participants, giving us both the responsibility and the benefit of our choices).

A Lithuanian representative in Vienna informed us that the Minister of Foreign Affairs, Mr Saudargas, Deputy Minister of Foreign Affairs, Mr Katkus, and a senior official at the Lithuanian Ministry of Foreign Affairs would like to be invited to the Summit. It seems to me that this request must be examined in light of what we know about the composition of the Soviet delegation, which will probably include about ten of the foreign ministers of the Soviet republics.

3. Topics for discussion during the closed debate

A first round of discussions identified the following topics:

— Economic development and/or economic assistance to Central and Eastern Europe (raised by Austria and seconded by Poland and the United States);

— The Mediterranean dimension of the CSCE (raised by Spain and seconded by Greece and Cyprus);

— The Gulf crisis (Malta asked a question on this subject but no specific delegation requested this topic to be included. The general feeling is, however, that it will most likely be addressed).

I would be grateful if the department could let me know by Thursday evening whether it would like other topics to be included, as a second round of discussions is scheduled for Friday.

4. Name of Czechoslovakia

The Czechoslovak delegation insisted on being referred to by its full name, the Czech and Slovak Federal Republic, including on table name signs.

The 34 agreed that if countries did not express a similar wish, their abbreviated name could be used on name signs, as was customary.

5. Lunches at the Élysée Palace and Quai d'Orsay

The delegations raised several points again (see my Diplomatic Telegram 929).

— Will heads of government who are not heads of delegations (as far as I know, this only concerns Turkey and Czechoslovakia) be invited to the Élysée Palace?

— What is the order of protocol for the Élysée Palace?

— Should a separate table be set up for "attendees" at the ministers' lunch?

– Who will lead the discussion between heads of delegations, and between ministers? I replied that the host of each of the lunches could give the floor to those who wished to speak. (C.C.). Signed: P. Morel./.

Noiville

11

Mr Morel, Head of the French delegation
   To the central administration

Diplomatic Telegram Vienna 1008   **15 November 1990.**

CSCE – Preparatory Committee for the Paris Summit. Meeting of the Twelve.

> Summary:
>
> Meeting of the Twelve: review of the draft speech by Jacques Delors, President of the Commission.

    1. At the meeting of the Heads of Delegation of the Twelve, the Presidency first raised the question of the dates for the first consultation meetings of the 34, to be set out in the Summit outcome document. Italy proposed that the session of the group of experts on administrative and financial matters, scheduled to take place in Vienna in mid-January, should be held on 14 and 15 January (the meeting of the CSCE group of experts of 8 January could therefore prepare the meeting). A brief exchange of views revealed that several delegations planned to appoint two experts in order to cover all the aspects to be addressed and to take into account the complete past of the CSCE. I recall that this meeting will be attended by a group of executive secretaries and designated directors, chaired by Mr Liederman (Austria), and with the participation of Mr Dessaux. The Presidency proposed 25 and 29 January for the first meeting of the Committee of Senior Officials in Prague, which would allow the Political Committee meeting on 15 and 16 January to prepare for it. As for participation, only Great Britain has indicated that it will most likely send its political director.

    I remind you that, for the first meeting of the Council of Ministers in Berlin, the FRG has proposed the dates of 19 and 20 June, which are set out in the draft document.

    2. The Presidency then distributed Mr Andreotti's draft speech, stating that it was being circulated at the same time by COREU. Given the urgency, and the opportunity offered by the extension of the work in Vienna, the Presidency indicated that it was considering holding a meeting in Vienna tomorrow, Thursday, to gather initial feedback more quickly.

    The representative of the Commission then circulated Mr Delors' draft speech (my fax No 170) with some very guarded comments to the effect that this text was not being submitted for review by the Twelve, whose reactions would only be forwarded to Brussels. During the exchange of views that ensued, Mr zu Rantzau considered that at least one third of the text went beyond the Commission's competence. For my part, I enquired about the degree of agreement within the council on Mr Lubbers' energy proposal, which Mr Delors very much supported. I then noted, with Luxembourg's support, that the formula of "European Energy

Charter" put forward by Mr Delors was in highly regrettable conflict with title envisaged for the Summit's outcome document. The Commission representative said that the Dutch proposal had been discussed at length at the General Affairs Council on Monday and that COREPER was now responsible for drafting a specific proposal. As for the title, our concern would be passed on to Brussels.

I'd be grateful for the Central Administration's feedback by 13:00 tomorrow. Signed: P. Morel./.

12

Elements for President Delors' speech at the CSCE Summit in Paris

Fax No 172 15 November 1990.

> Summary:
>
> Community position towards Central and Eastern Europe, draft European Energy Charter.

Since signing the Helsinki Final Act, the European Community has actively supported the CSCE process.

The idea of a Europe united in peace and the prospects of political, economic and cultural cooperation between the countries of Europe have largely contributed to a more stable environment and a more optimistic mood, despite the ongoing economic and political problems. The founding of the European Community has been a key element in the pursuit of this idea.

Indeed, is it not exemplary that an increasing number of countries in Europe, after the painful experience of bloody wars, are deliberately prepared to give up some of their sovereignty in order to create a new political structure? Long before the CSCE process was launched, they worked together to make Europe more stable, more peaceful, and more democratic. It was in the spirit of the ideas that were later incorporated into the Helsinki Final Act that these countries began to develop a common organization, attuned to the tradition of our cultures yet looking to the future, endowed with will and determination but devoid of any ambition to dominate.

The union of Europe remains a new idea and the Community is ready to embody it. Europe is taking action to move the Helsinki process forward. It is a reassuring move towards cooperation in all areas. Europe is thus following a logic of peace based on the recognition that the problems threatening human existence today will only be resolved by joint action. It is in this context that peaceful and enthusiastic crowds throughout Europe are calling for active participation in the process of change, contained in the great promise of the Helsinki Final Act. These crowds, which are responsible for great upheavals, have perhaps better understood than others that those who hesitate will be penalized by History.

In its determination to strengthen this process and on the basis of its responsibilities, the European Community lends its support to the CSCE. The Community has undertaken many projects to implement the letter and the spirit of the Helsinki process, in relation to the economy, the environment, information, science and technology. Over the past two years, this programme has expanded further. In the coming months, the Community will negotiate association agreements in the economic, political and cultural spheres with the countries of Central and Eastern Europe. A permanent, institutionalized dialogue at economic, political and cultural levels will be an essential element of these agreements. It will further strengthen the principles of multiparty democracy of pluralism, respect for human rights, and contribution as set out in the Bonn Declaration. Furthermore, as you are aware, the Commission coordinates the multilateral assistance of the Group of 24 to these countries.

On the basis of a request from the European Council, experts from the Commission and their Soviet counterparts, in close cooperation with international financial organizations, are examining the economic situation in the USSR and the possibility of external assistance for that country. The European Commission wants to make a significant effort to help the USSR in the difficult process of transition to a market economy and a pluralist democratic system.

In the spirit of the Helsinki Final Act, the Community has also made a substantial contribution to stability in Europe by helping the Germans to unite. We have warmly welcomed German unification. It highlights the dynamic evolution of the Community and demonstrates that we in Europe are all moving towards a reliable framework for peace and security.

While the Community is supporting developments in the East, it is also looking to other parts of Europe. Negotiations on a European Economic Area are entering their decisive phase.

On the other hand, developments in Central and Eastern Europe must not make us forget the situation with our southern neighbours – a community of history and destiny. Current events in the Gulf countries are threatening the stability of the region. Could the Helsinki process not serve as a model for giving our Arab friends the same stability and hopes that we have? The European Community, for its part, is determined to support our southern neighbours in their efforts to achieve economic prosperity and peace.

(Add a few words here on our transatlantic relations depending on developments in negotiations with the US and Canada on the Transatlantic Declaration).

Today, the Helsinki ideas are stronger than ever, but we cannot rest on our laurels. We must go further, not stop mid-way along the path of the CSCE process.

We in the European Community are constantly reflecting on the future of Europe. This is our duty and our daily work. That is why, today, I would like to make a concrete and pragmatic proposal that could contribute to resolving another urgent problem: that of energy.

My friend Ruud Lubbers has the merit of being the first to present this issue in a concrete form of political action. Let us see here, today, what we can do together realistically and practically to support this Dutch idea. This issue is part of a wider context which extends beyond the borders of Europe.

Let me explain: the central objective of the energy policy is to ensure security of supply under conditions that will improve economic competitiveness and the well-being of our citizens while at the same time creating a stable and beneficial situation for energy producers.

A European Energy Charter should create the necessary climate of confidence throughout the European continent to ensure that energy resources are developed and transported to places of consumption, both East and West.

It would contribute to the diversification of the international community's energy supply sources, thereby reducing tensions and stakes in other producing regions.

The Charter would thus establish the conditions, agreed by all signatory countries, that would govern industrial operations. This would, of course, encompass not only a non-discriminatory supply and distribution policy, but also the behaviour of the signatories in important areas related to energy production and consumption, including the issue of environmental protection, public security and respect for humanitarian principles, such as the free movement of persons or social protection.

The Charter would make it possible to highlight existing complementarities on the European continent between countries with resources, technologically advanced countries with expertise, and consumer markets. It would therefore contribute to an increased awareness of mutual responsibility when addressing issues related to energy supply and the environment.

The Community is ready to support the Dutch initiative to invite all CSCE countries to a Conference to draft such a Charter. The end result should not be a bureaucratic institution but rather a précis of the principles that the CSCE countries and the European institutions will apply in their energy policy.

Thus, the European Energy Charter could be accompanied by a series of protocols covering sectoral cooperation agreements relating to energy. Let me give some examples: a protocol on safety issues in civilian nuclear installations or a protocol on improving the efficiency of energy use and environmental protection, by limiting emissions from fuel cycle activities, for example. Other protocols could be established in the areas of long-distance natural gas transport, interconnection of electricity grids and the use of high-voltage networks.

I believe that in order to move Europe forward, we need to develop pragmatic and realistic approaches. This is what I have endeavoured to do. As we all know, the tasks before us are immense, especially for the European Community which fights every day to advance the unity of Europeans. As Robert Schuman said: "Europe will not be made all at once or according to a single plan. It will be built through concrete achievements which first create a de facto solidarity".

13

Mr Morel, Head of the French delegation
  To the central administration

Diplomatic Telegram Vienna 1029 17 November 1990.

CSCE - Preparatory Committee for the Paris Summit. Review of the Vienna Preparatory Committee. The Charter of Paris for a New Europe (1/3)

> Summary:
>
> Presentation of the Charter of Paris: introduction of the human dimension and broadening of security discussions to include all CSCE member states, beyond the Alliance and the Warsaw Pact.

As we strive to take a step back on the eve of the Summit, we must attempt a first critical reading of the outcome document being prepared by the Committee since the beginning of September.

1. The opening page avoids formal preambles and is more of a proclamation. Although unavoidably composite, it nevertheless establishes a certain register. The US delegation wanted sound bites, a simple message so that the following day's headlines would announce the irreversible end of the Cold War. Many European delegations, including ourselves, insisted on a strong reference to the restoration of historical continuity.

We, more than any other country, wanted to begin the first part with human rights, democracy and the rule of law, despite some reservations, including from the Germans, who wanted to exalt the will of the people. This is in fact the cornerstone of the Charter, because everything else stems from the solemn and precise affirmation of a community of values. By relentlessly insisting, with the support of the Twelve and particularly of Great Britain, on this essential starting point, we managed secure acceptance of the elements, if not the form, of a genuine "European democratic pact".

The chapter on friendly relations – taken from our draft "declaration" on friendly relations – was intended to correct the inevitable exercise between the member countries of the two alliances. It was not as strong as we would have liked, however the text of the 34 States balances out the declaration of the 22 States and specifies the new rules of conduct, highlighting the non-use of force, the peaceful settlement of disputes (accompanied by a decision in principle on the strengthening of mechanisms), the link between democracy and security (going beyond Principle VII), interdependence between States, and openness to the rest of the world.

This first part then ends with a specific mention of the new perceptions of security, desired by the new democracies, of German unity and the contribution of the North American States, and finally of the role of the United Nations.

2. The second part, on action lines, is organized around eight main themes, allowing us to leave behind the now obsolete framework of the three "baskets".

The priority given to the human dimension was justified, however the very substantial initial development on national minorities, with the announcement of the Geneva meeting next June, gives excessive importance to this theme, while the strengthening of the more general "human dimension" mechanism comes later, incorporating our idea of a college of personalities. Pushed by a powerful coalition (FRG, Italy, Switzerland, Hungary), it was perhaps in line with the spirit of the times. But this overly strong signal could lead to irredentism rather than the protection of the individuals and communities concerned. We will therefore have to be very vigilant in maintaining the necessary balance between the individual and the collective, which we reaffirmed on that occasion.

In fact, notwithstanding the CSCE's exemplary past in the field of human rights, this first chapter (and the Charter in general) marks a tremendous opening up which can only be managed through the systematic recourse to the now indispensable framework of the Council of Europe: if "Helsinki" was the Alpha, Strasbourg must be the Omega of all the citizens of Europe.

Significant progress has also been made in the area of security since we have obtained the inevitable but still postponed confirmation of the expansion of the parties to the negotiation from 22 to 34. The text remains vague, but, after the CFE Treaty, it marks the start of a new phase until Helsinki in 92. For the rest, a paragraph, requested by Yugoslavia and heavily reworked, deals with "other dangers" which "threaten the stability of our societies". As for the passage on the peaceful settlement of disputes, the most sensitive item in this part, it was unable to settle the vast debate that has opened up between the advocates of a legal approach, aimed at codifying inter-European relations (with compulsory recourse to third parties and judicial settlement), and those in favour of a more functional approach, through permanent consultations (within the framework of the future conflict prevention centre). (To be continued) Signed: P. Morel./.

Noiville

14

Mr Morel, Head of the French delegation
    To the central administration

Diplomatic Telegram Vienna 1030   **17 November 1990.**

CSCE – Preparatory Committee for the Paris Summit. Review of the Vienna Preparatory Committee. The Charter of Paris for a New Europe (2/3)

> Summary:
>
> The CSCE's cultural and economic ambitions ; the issue of migrants and the Mediterranean.

Faced with this dispute, which is somewhat reminiscent of the beginnings of the European Community, we pleaded alongside the British for a more pragmatic but immediate step forward, based on investigation, conciliation and arbitration, with the support of a college of elders. But everyone wanted to try their luck at the meeting of experts in Valletta in January, and we only managed to get this matter referred to the newly created Council of Ministers.

With regard to economic matters, the length of developments, which is rightly focused on the transition of former command economies, does little to hide the relative impotence of the CSCE in this area.

Although distinctly perceptible during contributions, but difficult to express in words, the fear among Central and Eastern European countries of a new division of Europe on an economic rather than ideological basis, is only partially evident. And, even more difficult to mention, the risk of large-scale migration due to poverty is ignored. The text ultimately recognizes that much will depend on close consultation between the relevant major organizations, with some emphasis on the EBRD.

The chapter on the environment is also provided, for good reasons. But here again, the CSCE must be content to be a "framework for the formulation of common commitments and objectives".

With regard to culture, long neglected by the CSCE because of the division of Europe, we insisted on launching a sort of catch-up at the Summit, and on setting some indisputable objectives: the Krakow meeting on heritage, the development of cultural centres and exchanges, and cooperation in the area of education.

With regard to migrant workers, it was agreed that this text should be independent of the economic chapter, a victory for the Yugoslavs and the Turks against the ever-reserved Germans.

With regard to the Mediterranean, it was probably not possible to take matters any further, but the reference to the Palma meeting in October, and to recent events, contributes to the consolidation of this long-time marginal element of the CSCE which is now poised to grow with it: although less than for the East, the text notes the risk of a growing gap with the South.

The final mention of non-governmental organizations is de rigueur, albeit somewhat outdated, despite various adjustments, in comparison with the recent "civil society" movements in Central and Eastern Europe.

3. The last and briefest part is the newest in respect of the CSCE, which for fifteen years remained a moral and political enterprise without a secular arm. The CSCE had to take the plunge, or risk petering out, while respecting the flexibility that has paradoxically strengthened the process over the past fifteen years. The participating States rightly chose incompleteness, since these "new structures", these "institutional arrangements" remain above all instruments of consultation and do not create a new international organization. But perhaps most interesting of all is that the negotiators endeavoured to strike a dynamic balance between the various bodies and procedures ("political" secretariat with general competence and "military" centre for confidence-building measures, ordinary and extraordinary meetings, governments and parliaments), and also to respect the rule of decentralization which at the same time consolidates and transposes the well-established CSCE practice of rotation that has been in place for the past 15 years.

With regard to the supplementary document, which essentially provides detailed instructions for the third part of the Charter, this is perhaps the most unexpected but most valuable achievement of the ultimately prolific Committee, since it underpins the ambitions, action lines and decisions of the "Charter" itself, justifying the choice of this demanding title. Here again, the negotiators have both exploited and transposed the CSCE *acquis* in order to give themselves the means to get the new course of events off the ground as soon as the Summit is over. (To be continued). Signed: P. Morel./.

15

Mr Morel, Head of the French delegation
   To the central administration

Diplomatic Telegram Vienna 1032   17 November 1990.

CSCE – Preparatory Committee for the Paris Summit. The delegations. (1/2)

Summary:

Review of the work of the Preparatory Committee: position of the different delegations (start).

   The striking feature of the behaviour of the different delegations making up the Preparatory Committee was diversity. The Twelve aside, great independence was shown, sometimes in an unpredictable manner. This was, of course, the case for the countries of Central and Eastern Europe, which were eager to take advantage of their new-found freedom of action. But this was also the case for the frequently divided neutrals and non-aligned, and even for several members of the Sixteen, including Canada, often closer to the community than the United States.

   1) The Twelve played a significant role in the Conference. They fulfilled their mandate to play "a leading role" in the negotiations. But the way in which they acted was inconsistent and at times provoked unfavourable reactions. Dynamic and imaginative in July and in early September, the Twelve then went through some difficult periods and, towards the end of the negotiations, could not avoid confrontation with the United States or irritating certain NNAs. This was probably inevitable in a transformed CSCE, where the traditional divisions no longer exist and the Twelve are therefore the only structured core group.

   The Italian Presidency was efficient and skilful, perhaps more in organizing the work of the Twelve and finding common positions than in promoting them among the 34. But, on the whole, the assessment of the Presidency has been very positive; it has mostly been ready to support our positions or to promote them among our partners.

   Among the latter, Germany has openly demonstrated its increased authority and weight since unification. Its primary concern was to secure the creation of the conflict prevention centre, the mandate for a meeting on minorities, and the adoption of the Declaration of the 22 States, promised to the Soviets. It insisted, sometimes excessively, on these points and demonstrated a certain lack of interest in many other subjects.

...

The British delegation, which had been very self-effacing at the beginning of the negotiations, gradually gained confidence, without however making any real proposals, apart from the illustration of human rights and its modest proposal on voluntary conciliation. It should be noted that the United Kingdom has been with us most of the time, including in our relations with the US delegation, with some hesitations that were quickly overcome.

The delegations from the Netherlands (rather unpredictable), Greece and, above all, Belgium also gave us valuable support, both vis-à-vis the Germans and the Americans. For their part, the Dutch focused mainly on the technical aspects of institutional matters (organization of the secretariat).

The other partners of the Twelve took little part in the discussions, with the Spanish only showing a particular interest in Mediterranean issues.

2) The Soviets were particularly discreet with regard to their own proposals, and extremely accommodating to all suggestions from other delegations. Their primary concern was to obtain in Vienna the most substantial declaration possible by the 22, and to confirm the creation of the conflict prevention centre. For the remainder, their instructions were clearly to facilitate all compromise formulas that would ensure agreement on the outcome document.

3) By contrast, the US delegation was very active and ready to challenge the Twelve at any time. The general climate of relations between the Sixteen and the Twelve has been essentially quite good, despite brief but intense periods of confrontation. The negotiations of the last few days have in fact been between the Americans, supported by Turkey, on the one hand, and the members of the community, often supported by the Canadians and Norwegians, on the other. (GF). (To be continued). Signed P. Morel./.

Noiville

16

Mr Morel, Head of the French delegation
   To the central administration

Diplomatic Telegram Vienna 1033   *17 November 1990.*

CSCE – Preparatory Committee for the Paris Summit. The delegations (2/2)

> Summary:
>
> Review of the work of the Preparatory Committee: position of the different delegations (end).

4) The delegations of the main Central and Eastern European countries continued to engage in discussions until the end, but it must be said that they did not really have coherent or convincing overall plans. Hungary positioned itself as an active intermediary in all areas, while the Czechoslovak delegation was mainly concerned, not always deftly, with the future headquarters of the CSCE Secretariat in Prague, and the Poles focused on important but specialized issues (borders, visas, preparation of the Krakow cultural seminar, elections office).

5) The four neutral delegations played coordination roles under very varying conditions. The Swedish representative, coordinator of the first part of the document, managed slowly but surely to lead all 34 states towards a consensus text without having to defend national positions. In contrast, the Swiss coordinator of the second part, despite his skill, did not manage to resolve two serious issues in his text – linked to our proposal on the CSCE High Council – until the final hour. Switzerland's specific position on the human dimension issues and the peaceful settlement of disputes actually complicated the search for solutions. But it was the Finnish coordinator who found himself in the most difficult situation. His responsibility was to develop the permanent institutions of the CSCE, while his authorities' main concern was clearly to avoid a strong commitment in this area before the next Summit meeting in Helsinki in 1992. As for the Austrian coordinator, he only intervened at the last minute for the assembly of the overall document, aligning himself almost systematically with the positions of the Twelve.

There can be little doubt that the coordination role traditionally performed by the neutrals is coming to an end. The difficulties caused by the Finnish, and the creation of semi-clandestine workshops where interested delegations drafted texts in parallel with the coordinators' groups, confirm the inevitable shift in the CSCE's working methods. (GF). Signed: P. Morel./.

Noiville

17

Mr Morel, Head of the French delegation
    To the central administration

Diplomatic Telegram Vienna 1034   **17 November 1990.**

CSCE – Preparatory Committee for the Paris Summit. Closing plenary session

> Summary:
>
> Adoption of the text of the Charter of Paris by consensus, in accordance with CSCE practice.

The Preparatory Committee's final plenary session was held in the evening of 17 November and continued briefly on Saturday morning, after being adjourned from midnight to 9:00 a.m.

The draft document entitled "Charter of Paris for a New Europe" and the draft supplementary document were adopted by consensus ad referendum. The United States delegation reserved the right to confirm its agreement on Saturday morning, pending conclusion of the negotiations on CSBMs, which, in its view, was a precondition for the establishment of the conflict prevention centre.

The President of the session read out a statement for the journal of the day specifying, at the request of the German delegation, that the first Council of Foreign Ministers had been invited to take place in Berlin on 19 to 21 June 1991. Formal agreement on these dates is expected to be reached in Paris.

As set out in the scenario developed for the creation of a CSCE parliamentary assembly, the Spanish delegate also confirmed that Mr Gonzalez would announce in Paris that the Spanish parliament would invite the parliaments of participating States to a first joint meeting of CSCE parliamentarians in early 1991.

I then underlined the ambitious and concrete nature of the draft that had been completed. While the experience of recent days demonstrated the virtues and shortcomings of consensus, I wanted to emphasize above all that the baskets had been superseded by a thematic approach, reflecting the new spirit of the CSCE with a priority on substance and common references. As a founding innovation, we had provided the CSCE with flexible institutions. Now we had to face, with confidence, a triple test: endorsement by our authorities, acceptance by the public, the sanction of time...

In conclusion, I reminded those present of the formula used by the President of the Republic in 1975 when the Helsinki Final Act was adopted, lest it be forgotten that there was nothing in the Charter of Paris that gave recognition to situations that had not already been recognized. The Soviet delegation had been informed in advance of this reference to the Baltic States, which are grouped under the Soviet Union in the CFE Treaty.

The Ambassador of Canada provided his interpretation of the sentence dealing with expansion of the human dimension mechanism, which refers to the services of experts and a panel of prominent figures. Canada did consider it to be a non-exclusive procedure, to be defined more fully at the Moscow conference.

Several delegations (United States, USSR, Switzerland, Netherlands, Italy, Czechoslovakia and Romania) took the floor to welcome the approved documents in general terms and to underline the historic nature of the Paris Summit, which would mark a turning point for the CSCE and give it a new dimension.

On Saturday morning, the few who attended gave their full approval of both draft documents, however several delegations made various interpretative statements. The representative of Finland pointed out that the next meeting CSCE follow-up meeting, to be held in Helsinki in 1992, should be opened at ministerial level, as was customary. In view of the creation of a Council of Ministers of the 34, within the framework of the political consultation mechanism established by the Paris Summit, he indicated that his authorities wanted the Council to meet as such at the opening of the Helsinki meeting.

For his part, the Spanish delegate recalled, in an interpretative statement, that the formulas negotiated in Vienna did not prejudice the case of Gibraltar and described the "colonial" nature of the situation. The delegation of the United Kingdom replied that the CSCE was not the appropriate forum to address this issue, which should be dealt with bilaterally. Lively exchanges ensued between the two delegations on the subject. The representatives of Turkey and Greece also set out their respective positions on the Cyprus question. (AS/GF). Signed. P. Morel./.

Noiville

18

Mr Plaisant, Head of the French Delegation to the CSCE
To the central administration

Diplomatic Telegram DMST Vienna 1030   17 November 1990.

Vienna Document 1990 of the Negotiations on Confidence and Security Building Measures

> Summary:
>
> Conclusion of the negotiation of the Treaty on Conventional Armed Forces.

The negotiators of the thirty-four participating States managed, not without several night sessions in the last few days, to draft the substantive document they were asked to prepare for the Summit.

This final rush was to some extent the payback for a certain languor that had characterized the negotiation for twenty months.

From the outset, it was a somewhat poor relation in comparison with the 23-state negotiation on conventional armed forces, which had the prestige of being unprecedented. The CSBM negotiation followed on from the Stockholm negotiation (1984-1986), which was also the first of its kind. As a result, it lacked a little originality. It aimed to improve the measures adopted in Stockholm (e.g. by adopting more demanding parameters) and to develop new ones. On this point, there was a sense that the experts' imagination had dried up, unless we were to dig up the old ammunition that the Warsaw Pact had brought out for the occasion, such as demilitarized geographical zones. It also proved difficult to find new confidence- and security-building measures without encroaching on the area of disarmament, and without pushing some countries, starting with the United States, beyond their limits.

*

From the outset it was obvious that the differences would centre around two points:

– The first three measures proposed by the Sixteen: information on air-land forces, information on new deployments, and a system of "random evaluation" of this exchange of information. The exchange of information had been the hobbyhorse of the Sixteen in Stockholm, but they had ultimately failed to obtain it because the USSR saw it as a legal form of espionage. This time, in Vienna, the principle was accepted fairly quickly. But the negotiations immediately stumbled over the scope of the exchange: the USSR made the inclusion of naval forces a prerequisite;

– The naval issue was a common thread in all discussions. As we are aware, the Madrid mandate, as interpreted by the Sixteen, excludes any naval activity that is not functionally linked to land-based activity in the area. Several allies were inclined to seek a compromise on this point, but the United States stood firm. The result was that there was a stalemate until 13 November when the head of the Soviet delegation agreed to negotiate genuinely on a compromise document on information without explicit reference to naval forces.

The reason the USSR finally conceded, as in Stockholm, was that the Sixteen argued that the absence of CSBMs on information would deprive the planned conflict prevention centre (CPC) – to which the USSR and Germany were also committed – of all substance.

In the meantime, the consultations had dragged on for months, progressing line by line and requiring long efforts. There were several reasons for this:

– The inherent slowness of the CSCE process involving decision by consensus, i.e. the veto, and also the habit of leaving time to do the work;

– The attitude of the neutrals, which should have collectively taken the lead; some of them (Switzerland) were reluctant to commit, and others (Finland, of course) were afraid of anticipating the Helsinki conference;

– Last but not least, the attitude of some of the Sixteen which, after the Atlantic Summit in Brussels in May 1989, stalled the 35-state negotiations on the pretext of giving priority to the CFE Treaty. The attitude of France, followed by the FRG, was decisive in relaunching the movement at the beginning of 1990.

*

The document to be submitted to the Heads of State and Government satisfies our requirements. It includes information measures with parameters that are undoubtedly less than what we wanted, but which are nevertheless satisfactory. It includes 15 measures out of the 18 in our original proposals, of which the main one is undoubtedly the famous "measure 15" on "unusual military activities", which in other words aims to institute consultation mechanisms in the event of a threat of war. Other measures include the annual evaluation meetings associated with the future CPC, measures to prevent dangerous military incidents, and the establishment of a communications network. There is no mention of the "naval" issue, except that the proposals already on the table may be the subject of subsequent negotiations, which goes without saying.

Let me conclude by pointing out that the French representation has been very active throughout these negotiations, successfully working to avoid a stalemate, and on several occasions suggesting ideas that ultimately provided a way out of an impasse./.

Plaisant

19

Mr Morel, Head of the French delegation
To the central administration

Diplomatic Telegram DMST Vienna 1030   **17 November 1990.**

CSCE – Preparatory Committee for the Paris Summit. Emergency meeting mechanism (1/2)

Summary:

Final negotiations before the Paris Summit.

I refer to my Diplomatic Telegram No 1016.

On the last day of the Preparatory Committee's work, the absence of new instructions for the United States delegation on the question of the mechanism for emergency meetings led the Twelve to present the latest version of their draft at a meeting of the thirty-four participating States (see fax No 185). Mr Maresca had previously announced to his partners of the Sixteen that he intended to challenge point 5 relating to the method of convening such meetings.

The 34 were surprised to learn of the presentation by the Yugoslav delegation, acting on instruction, of a proposal to replace all the provisions relating to the emergency mechanism contained in the coordinator's text with a single sentence: "the committee of senior officials will discuss the establishment of an emergency mechanism and prepare proposals to this aim to the council of ministers of foreign affairs, in order to prepare recommendations for the Helsinki follow-up meeting".

Obviously contested by the Twelve, whose text had received very strong support from delegations that were more reserved about the previous version of the draft (Sweden and Turkey in particular), this suggestion was supported by the United States delegation. It is true that the sentence put forward by the Yugoslavs used the very words of a proposal by the US delegation to the Sixteen. At the same time, the United States delegation proposed to amend point 5 of the text of the Twelve by providing that the Chairman of the Committee of Senior Officials would seek the consensus of participating States before convening an emergency meeting.

The coordinator then suggested that these three alternative positions should be presented in brackets, whereupon I intervened to point out that this was in fact a major political issue. I demonstrated once again how the text of the Twelve, which now took into account the concerns expressed by some, was a key element of effective political consultations. Furthermore, I recalled that the CSCE process already had two exceptions to the consensus rule, namely measure 15 and the human dimension mechanism. Conversely, the American and Yugoslav proposals could not convince us: the latter would result in the emergency mechanism being detached from the institutional structure. As for the American set-up, it would paradoxically make it more difficult to convene an emergency meeting than an ordinary meeting, as the former would be subject to "clarification".

A working group brought together interested delegations to explore ways of reaching a compromise.

...

Straight away, Mr Maresca proposed to replace all the provisions of paragraph c of the supplementary document on the emergency mechanism with a sentence designed to preserve the possibility of agreement at ministerial level, ideally as early as Paris, if possible, or if not at a later date.

During the exchanges, it became increasingly clear that the United States' objection to the position put forward by the Twelve, which in its latest form had received the support of almost all delegations in the morning, was much more radical than its presentation suggested. Despite several invitations from the coordinator, in line with my suggestions, Mr Maresca stubbornly declared that he was unable to accept – either in brackets or even as an alternative statement by the President of the day – the inclusion of the text of the Twelve. The mere repetition of his proposed amendment to the text that morning, aimed at reintroducing the rule of consensus for convening emergency meetings, could not satisfy him if he was unable to endorse an approach that seemed to him to give status to this text. He was not in a position to propose a specific US text on this subject either.

It was not possible in these circumstances to keep the mechanism developed by the Twelve, even as guidelines for the Ministers' consideration of the matter.

However, I stressed the need, given the significance of this mechanism for the credibility of future political consultations as part of the CSCE process, to explicitly announce in the main document that the issue remained under consideration by Ministers in Council. Indeed, the existing sentence, which referred in a very general way to the possibility of additional meetings, was insufficient. There was a clear need for the possibility to convene meetings without seeking prior consensus. My suggestion to add a second sentence to supplement the text to this effect was finally accepted. (MH) (To be continued). Signed P. Morel./.

Michel FOUCHER
CONCLUSION

Thirty years after the signing of the Charter of Paris for a New Europe, contributors and researchers asked to contribute by the Archives Directorate of the Ministry for Europe and Foreign Affairs seem to agree on the importance of this text which is still an important reference. It set out an ideal objective to have, if not achieve, and explained the ways to do this in detail, and above all in a European framework.

The issue of how to achieve a genuine "Concert of Europe" across the whole continent still needs to be addressed. The fact that a satisfactory response has not been found in the past three decades does not invalidate the original intention or the proposals it puts forward. The time of history passes slowly, between two bifurcations – and the end of the Cold War was a major one – and it is important to accept that. Declaring failure is the predictable reaction of impatient people who do not realize history takes time.

President François Mitterrand was keenly aware that a hand needed to be extended to the other part of Europe. He assessed the weaknesses, which were undoubtedly inevitable, and the settlements of the First World War. He knew that the United States' wish to re-incorporate Germany into the European game after 1945, once the totalitarian Nazi regime was defeated, made it possible, on the contrary, to lay down more solid foundations for a more lasting European order. He therefore believed it was necessary to involve Russia in a new continent-wide cooperative scheme and not to treat it as a defeated country as it was emerging from an ideological and strategic confrontation that had left it in ruins.

The ambitious goal of France, which was reiterated at the European Confederation meeting in Prague following on from the Charter of Paris, was sound. But its lengthy reach undoubtedly underestimated the weight of the painful pasts in former Eastern Europe, explaining the pressing need for a guarantee of last resort – in reality American – which would find its spontaneous response in the accelerated extension of the area of US influence. The United States considered itself the winner of the geostrategic bifurcation of 1989-1990: Washington did not have the historic or cultural sensitivity of Paris, nor the intention to accompany an initial and fragile transition in Russia.

Although German reunification was achieved within a European framework, as François Mitterrand wished, although integration in the institutional bodies encouraged in Central Europe the signature of bilateral agreements recognizing the outlines of existing borders and offering guarantees to national minorities, before the act of accession to the European Union and although European and transatlantic institutions offered a pre-existing framework of stability, it is important to highlight that several signatories did not honour their commitments.

Before pledging support for the Charter, the United States, in a position of strength, demanded a Treaty on Conventional Armed Forces be signed, which was achieved an hour before the start of the summit. More than a new security architecture, it was a sign that an extension of NATO was coming. And President Bush Senior clearly did not wish for Gorbachev to succeed and was supported by London, opposing the opinion of Paris and Bonn. In December 1991, USSR collapsed, of its own doing and upon itself, as a geopolitical reality.

In the years that followed, several signatories of the Charter of Paris did not take into account the analysis of France. The principles relating to national borders and minorities, signed by the delegation of Yugoslavia, were immediately flouted by nationalist leaders anxious to fight. Russia adhered to the Charter to an even lesser degree and resorted to the long-used method of frozen conflicts inspired by Stalin nationality policy: Georgia in the summer of 2008, Transistria from the start, Crimea and Eastern Ukraine, not to mention the current plan of merging with Belarus.

Ambassador Pierre Morel, who worked on the Charter in the field in France's diplomatic representation to the CSCE in Vienna, has laboured tirelessly on the implementation of the Minsk agreements regarding Ukraine because he believes that in 2020, European security is at stake, just as it was in 1990. This work to overcome what went wrong – the last words in Hubert Védrine's interview – in the relationship with Russia illustrates a remarkable continuity of France's diplomatic commitment towards a great peaceful Europe and that is capable of settling disputes resulting from the bifurcation of 1990.

And as Jean Musitelli – who was in daily contact with Pierre Morel during that time – indicated, the Charter outlined "one great Europe based on truly shared values and interests". And this is still the case. However, one can agree that the establishment of a democratic regime in Russia would make things easier.

The "Magna Carta of Freedom" ideal mentioned by Nicolas Badalassi remains, for it was clearly set out in 1990. But European history has imposed its implacable long duration and collision of national trajectories. Time is needed for the most lucid ideas to spread. In this regard, the Charter is not just a text of valuable archives for interested historians but also a reference document for designing the future of the continent.

ANNEXES

Paris Summit Programme

Friday, 16 November 1990

CSCE
Executive Secretariat
Press Department

PARIS SUMMIT

PROGRAMME

Monday, 19 November 1990

9:00 to 10:00	ÉLYSÉE PALACE
	Signature of the Treaty on Conventional Armed Forces and the Joint Declaration of the 22 Member States of the North Atlantic Pact and the Warsaw Pact.
11:00 to 11:45	Official Opening Session of the Paris Summit by the President of the French Republic. Address by the President of the French Republic.
	Address by the United Nations Secretary-General.
13:00	Lunch hosted by the President of the Republic for Heads of State and Government.
15:00 to 18:30	Second Plenary Session chaired by Helmut KOHL, Chancellor of the Federal Republic of Germany.

                              <u>15 speeches</u> (list subject to changes),
                                1 - Canada
                                2 - 3 - Italy – European Community
                                4 - Malta
                                5 - United States of America
                                6 - Denmark
                                7 - Union of Soviet Socialist Republics
                                8 - Czech and Slovak Federative Republic
                                9 - Switzerland
                                10 - Portugal
                                11 - Great Britain

ANNEXES

          12 - Sweden
          13 - Netherlands
          14 - Holy See
          15 - Turkey

19:00   Reception at the Palais de Chaillot, Musée des Monuments Historiques.

Tuesday, 20 November 1990

Third Plenary Session of the Summit under the Presidency of Gabriele Gatti, Head of the Government of San Marino

          <u>12 speeches</u> (list subject to changes)
          16 - Ireland
          17 - Poland
          18 - Hungary
          19 - Yugoslavia
          20 - Spain
          21 - Greece
          22 - Iceland
          23 - Austria
          24 - Cyprus
          25 - Belgium
          26 - Germany
          27 - Norway

Fourth Plenary Session chaired by Turgut OZAL, President of the Republic of Turkey.

          <u>8 speeches</u> (list subject to changes)
          28 - Romania
          29 - San Marino
          30 - Finland
          31 - Monaco
          32 - Luxembourg
          33 - Liechtenstein
          34 - Bulgaria

17:00 to 18:30   Closed session.

21:00 to 23:30   Gala event at Versailles and a ballet at the Opéra Royal with Patrice DUPOND.

Wednesday, 21 November 1990

10:00 to 11:15   Fifth Plenary Session under the Presidency of Francois Mitterrand, President of the French Republic.

                  Signature of the Final Act of the Paris Summit and closing speech of the President of the French Republic.

Charter of Paris for a new Europe
(Paris, 19-21 November 1990)

Meeting of the Heads of State or Government of the participating States of the Conference on Security and Co-operation in Europe (CSCE): Austria, Belgium, Bulgaria, Canada, Cyprus, Czech and Slovak Federal Republic, Denmark, Finland, France, Germany, Greece, Holy See, Hungary, Iceland, Ireland, Italy- European Community, Liechtenstein, Luxembourg, Malta, Monaco, Netherlands, Norway, Poland, Portugal, Romania, San Marino, Spain, Sweden, Switzerland, Turkey, Union of Soviet Socialist Republics, United Kingdom, United States of America and Yugoslavia.

A new era of Democracy, Peace and Unity

We, the Heads of State or Government of the States participating in the Conference on Security and Co-operation in Europe, have assembled in Paris at a time of profound change and historic expectations. The era of confrontation and division of Europe has ended. We declare that henceforth our, relations will be founded on respect and co-operation.

Europe is liberating itself from the legacy of the past. The courage of men and women, the strength of the will of the peoples and the power of the ideas of the Helsinki Final Act have opened a new era of democracy, peace and unity in Europe.

Ours is a time for fulfilling the hopes and expectations our peoples have cherished for decades: steadfast commitment to democracy based on human rights and fundamental freedoms; prosperity through economic liberty and social justice; and equal security for all our countries.

The Ten Principles of the Final Act will guide us towards this ambitious future, just as they have lighted our way towards better relations for the past fifteen years. Full implementation of all CSCE commitments must form the basis for the initiatives we are now taking to enable our nations to live in accordance with their aspirations.

Human Rights, Democracy and Rule of Law

We undertake to build, consolidate and strengthen democracy as the only system of government of our nations. In this endeavour, we will abide by the following:

Human rights and fundamental freedoms are the birthright of all human beings, are inalienable and are guaranteed by law. Their protection and promotion is the first responsibility of government. Respect for them is an essential safeguard against an over-mighty State. Their observance and full exercise are the foundation of freedom, justice and peace.

Democratic government is based on the will of the people, expressed regularly through free and fair elections. Democracy has as its foundation respect for the human person and the rule of law. Democracy is the best safeguard of freedom of expression, tolerance of all groups of society, and equality of opportunity for each person.

Democracy, with its representative and pluralist character, entails accountability to the electorate, the obligation of public authorities to comply with the law and justice administered impartially. No one will be above the law.

We affirm that, without discrimination, every individual has the right to freedom of thought, conscience and religion or belief,
- freedom of expression,
- freedom of association and peaceful assembly,
- freedom of movement;

no one will be:
- subject to arbitrary arrest or detention,
- subject to torture or other cruel, inhuman or degrading treatment or punishment;

everyone also has the right:
- to know and act upon his rights,
- to participate in free and fair elections,
- to fair and public trial if charged with an offence,
- to own property alone or in association and to exercise individual enterprise,
- to enjoy his economic, social and cultural rights.

We affirm that the ethnic, cultural, linguistic and religious identity of national minorities will be protected and that persons belonging to national minorities have the right freely to express, preserve and develop that identity without any discrimination and in full equality before the law.

We will ensure that everyone will enjoy recourse to effective remedies, national or international, against any violation of his rights.

Full respect for these precepts is the bedrock on which we will seek to construct the new Europe.

Our States will co-operate and support each other with the aim of making democratic gains irreversible.

Economic Liberty and Responsibility

Economic liberty, social justice and environmental responsibility are indispensable for prosperity.

The free will of the individual, exercised in democracy and protected by the rule of law, forms the necessary basis for successful economic and social development. We will promote economic activity which respects and upholds human dignity.

Freedom and political pluralism are necessary elements in our common objective of developing market economies towards sustainable economic growth, prosperity, social justice, expanding employment and efficient use of economic resources. The success of the transition to market economy by countries making efforts to this effect is important and in the interest of us all. It will enable us to share a higher level of prosperity which is our common objective. We will co-operate to this end.

Preservation of the environment is a shared responsibility of all our nations. While supporting national and regional efforts in this field, we must also look to the pressing need for joint action on a wider scale.

Friendly Relations among Participating States

Now that a new era is dawning in Europe, we are determined to expand and strengthen friendly relations and co-operation among the States of Europe, the United States of America and Canada, and to promote friendship among our peoples.

To uphold and promote democracy, peace and unity in Europe, we solemnly pledge our full commitment to the Ten Principles of the Helsinki Final Act. We affirm the continuing validity of the Ten Principles and our determination to put them into practice. All the Principles apply equally and unreservedly, each of them being interpreted taking into account the others. They form the basis for our relations.

In accordance with our obligations under the Charter of the United Nations and commitments under the Helsinki Final Act, we renew our pledge to refrain from the threat or use of force against the territorial integrity or political independence of any State, or from acting in any other manner inconsistent with the principles or purposes of those documents. We recall that non-compliance with obligations under the Charter of the United Nations constitutes a violation of international law.

We reaffirm our commitment to settle disputes by peaceful means. We decide to develop mechanisms for the prevention and resolution of conflicts among the participating States.

With the ending of the division of Europe, we will strive for a new quality in our security relations while fully respecting each other's freedom of choice in that respect. Security is indivisible and the security of every participating State is inseparably linked to that of all the others. We therefore pledge to co-operate in strengthening confidence and security among us and in promoting arms control and disarmament.

We welcome the Joint Declaration of Twenty-Two States on the improvement of their relations.

Our relations will rest on our common adherence to democratic values and to human rights and fundamental freedoms. We are convinced that in order to strengthen peace and security among our States, the advancement of democracy, and respect for and effective exercise of human rights, are indispensable. We reaffirm the equal rights of peoples and their right to self-determination in conformity with the Charter of the United Nations and with the relevant norms of international law, including those relating to territorial integrity of States.

We are determined to enhance political consultation and to widen co-operation to solve economic, social, environmental, cultural and humanitarian problems. This common resolve and our growing interdependence will help to overcome the mistrust of decades, to increase stability and to build a united Europe.

We want Europe to be a source of peace, open to dialogue and to co-operation with other countries, welcoming exchanges and involved in the search for common responses to the challenges of the future.

Security

Friendly relations among us will benefit from the consolidation of democracy and improved security.

We welcome the signature of the Treaty on Conventional Armed Forces in Europe by twenty-two participating States, which will lead to lower levels of armed forces. We endorse the adoption of a substantial new set of Confidence- and Security-building Measures which will lead to increased transparency and confidence among all participating States. These are important steps towards enhanced stability and security in Europe.

The unprecedented reduction in armed forces resulting from the Treaty on Conventional Armed Forces in Europe, together with new approaches to security and co-operation within the CSCE process, will lead to a new perception of security in Europe and a new dimension in our relations. In this context we fully recognize the freedom of States to choose their own security arrangements.

Unity

Europe whole and free is calling for a new beginning. We invite our peoples to join in this great endeavour.

We note with great satisfaction the Treaty on the Final Settlement with respect to Germany signed in Moscow on 12 September 1990 and sincerely welcome the fact that the German people have united to become one State in accordance with the principles of the Final Act of the Conference on Security and Co-operation in Europe and in full accord with their neighbours. The establishment of the national unity of Germany is an important contribution to a just and lasting order of peace for a united, democratic Europe aware of its responsibility for stability, peace and co-operation.

The participation of both North American and European States is a fundamental characteristic of the CSCE; it underlies its past achievements and is essential to the future of the CSCE process. An abiding adherence to shared values and our common heritage are the ties which bind us together. With all the rich diversity of our nations, we are united in our commitment to expand our co-operation in all fields. The challenges confronting us can only be met by common action, co-operation and solidarity.

The CSCE and the World

The destiny of our nations is linked to that of all other nations. We support fully the United Nations and the enhancement of its role in promoting international peace, security and justice. We reaffirm our commitment to the principles and purposes of the United Nations as enshrined in the Charter and condemn all violations of these principles. We recognize with satisfaction the growing role of the United Nations in world affairs and its increasing effectiveness, fostered by the improvement in relations among our States.

Aware of the dire needs of a great part of the world, we commit ourselves to solidarity with all other countries. Therefore, we issue a call from Paris today to all the nations of the world. We stand ready to join with any and all States in common efforts to protect and advance the community of fundamental human values.

Guidelines for the future

Proceeding from our firm commitment to the full implementation of all CSCE principles and provisions, we now resolve to give a new impetus to a balanced and comprehensive development of our co-operation in order to address the needs and aspirations of out peoples.

Human Dimension

We declare our respect for human rights and fundamental freedoms to be irrevocable. We will fully implement and build upon the provisions relating to the human dimension of the CSCE.

Proceeding from the Document of the Copenhagen Meeting of the Conference on the Human Dimension, we will cooperate to strengthen democratic institutions and to promote the application of the rule of law. To that end, we decide to convene a seminar of experts in Oslo from 4 to 15 November 1991.

Determined to foster the rich contribution of national minorities to the life of our societies, we undertake further to improve their situation. We reaffirm our deep conviction that friendly relations among our peoples, as well as peace, justice, stability and democracy, require that the ethnic, cultural, linguistic and religious identity of national minorities be protected and conditions for the promotion of that identity be created. We declare that questions related to national minorities can only be satisfactorily resolved in a democratic political framework. We further acknowledge that the rights of persons belonging to national minorities must be fully respected as part of universal human rights. Being aware of the urgent need for increased cooperation on, as well as better protection of, national minorities, we decide to convene a meeting of experts on national minorities to be held in Geneva from 1 to 19 July 1991.

We express our determination to combat all forms of racial and ethnic hatred, antisemitism, xenophobia and discrimination against anyone as well as persecution on religious and ideological grounds.

In accordance with our CSCE commitments, we stress that free movement and contacts among our citizens as well as the free flow of information and ideas are crucial for the maintenance and development of free societies and flourishing cultures. We welcome increased tourism and visits among our countries.

The human dimension mechanism has proved its usefulness, and we are consequently determined to expand it to include new procedures involving, *inter alia*, the services of experts or a roster of eminent persons experienced in human rights issues which could be raised under the mechanism. We shall provide, in the context of the mechanism, for individuals to be involved in the protection of their rights. Therefore, we undertake to develop further our commitments in this respect, in particular at the Moscow Meeting of the Conference on the Human Dimension, without prejudice to obligations under existing international instruments to which our States may be parties.

We recognize the important contribution of the Council of Europe to the promotion of human rights and the principles of democracy and the rule of law as well as to the development of cultural co-operation. We welcome moves by several participating States to join the Council of Europe and adhere to its European Convention on Human Rights. We welcome as well the readiness of the Council of Europe to make its experience available to the CSCE.

Security

The changing political and military environment in Europe opens new possibilities for common efforts in the field of military security. We will build on the important achievements attained in the Treaty on Conventional Armed Forces in Europe and in the Negotiations on Confidence- and Security-building Measures. We undertake to continue the CSBM negotiations under the same mandate, and to seek to conclude them no later than the Follow-up Meeting of the CSCE to be held in Helsinki in 1992. We also welcome the decision of the participating States concerned to continue the CFE negotiation under the same mandate and to seek to conclude it no later than the Helsinki Follow-up Meeting. Following a period for national preparations, we look forward to a more structured co-operation among all participating States on security matters, and to discussions and consultations among the thirty-four participating States aimed at establishing by 1992, from the conclusion of the Helsinki Follow-up Meeting, new negotiations on disarmament and confidence and security building open to all participating States.

We call for the earliest possible conclusion of the Convention on an effectively verifiable, global and comprehensive ban on chemical weapons, and we intend to be original signatories to it.

We reaffirm the importance of the Open Skies initiative and call for the successful conclusion of the negotiations as soon as possible.

Although the threat of conflict in Europe has diminished, other dangers threaten the stability of our societies. We are determined to co-operate in defending democratic institutions against activities which violate the independence, sovereign equality or territorial integrity of the participating States. These include illegal activities involving outside pressure, coercion and subversion.

We unreservedly condemn, as criminal, all acts, methods and practices of terrorism and express our determination to work for its eradication both bilaterally and through multilateral co-operation. We will also join together in combating illicit trafficking in drugs.

Being aware that an essential complement to the duty of States to refrain from the threat or use of force is the peaceful settlement of disputes, both being essential factors for the maintenance and consolidation of international peace and security, we will not only seek effective ways of preventing, through political means, conflicts which may yet emerge, but also define, in conformity with international law, appropriate mechanisms for the peaceful resolution of any disputes which may arise. Accordingly, we undertake to seek new forms of co-operation in this area, in particular a range of methods for the peaceful settlement of disputes, including mandatory third-party involvement. We stress that full use should be made in this context of the opportunity of the Meeting on the Peaceful Settlement of Disputes which will be convened in Valletta at the beginning of 1991. The Council of Ministers for Foreign Affairs will take into account the Report of the Valletta Meeting.

Economic Co-operation

We stress that economic co-operation based on market economy constitutes an essential element of our relations and will be instrumental in the construction of a prosperous and united Europe. Democratic institutions and economic liberty foster economic and social progress, as recognized in the Document of the Bonn Conference on Economic Co-operation, the results of which we strongly support.

We underline that co-operation in the economic field, science and technology is now an important pillar of the CSCE. The participating States should periodically review progress and give new impulses in these fields.

We are convinced that our overall economic co-operation should be expanded, free enterprise encouraged and trade increased and diversified according to GATT rules. We will promote social justice and progress and further the welfare of our peoples. We recognize in this context the importance of effective policies to address the problem of unemployment.

We reaffirm the need to continue to support democratic countries in transition towards the establishment of market economy and the creation of the basis for self-sustained economic and social growth, as already undertaken by the Group of twenty-four countries. We further underline the necessity of their increased integration, involving the acceptance of disciplines as well as benefits, into the international economic and financial system.

We consider that increased emphasis on economic co-operation within the CSCE process should take into account the interests of developing participating States.

We recall the link between respect for and promotion of human rights and fundamental freedoms and scientific progress. Co-operation in the field of science and technology will play an essential role in economic and social development. Therefore, it must evolve towards a greater sharing of appropriate scientific and technological information and knowledge with a view to overcoming the technological gap which exists among the participating States. We further encourage the participating States to work together in order to develop human potential and the spirit of free enterprise.

We are determined to give the necessary impetus to co-operation among our States in the fields of energy, transport and tourism for economic and social development. We welcome, in particular, practical steps to create optimal conditions for the economic and rational development of energy resources, with due regard for environmental considerations.

We recognize the important role of the European Community in the political and economic development of Europe. International economic organizations such as the United Nations Economic Commission for Europe (ECE), the Bretton Woods Institutions, the Organisation for Economic Co-operation and Development (ECD), the European Free Trade Association (EFTA) and the International Chamber of Commerce (ICC) also have a significant task in promoting economic co-operation, which will be further enhanced by the establishment of the European Bank for Reconstruction and Development (EBRD). In order to pursue our objectives, we stress the necessity for effective co-ordination of the activities of these organizations and emphasize the need to find methods for all our States to take part in these activities.

Environment

We recognize the urgent need to tackle the problems of the environment and the importance of individual and co-operative efforts in this area. We pledge to intensify our endeavours to protect and improve our environment in order to restore and maintain a sound ecological balance in air, water and soil. Therefore, we are determined to make full use of the CSCE as a framework for the formulation of common environmental commitments and objectives, and thus to pursue the work reflected in the Report of the Sofia Meeting on the Protection of the Environment.

We emphasize the significant role of a well-informed society in enabling the public and individuals to take initiatives to improve the environment. To this end, we commit ourselves to promoting public awareness and education on the environment as well as the public reporting of the environmental impact of policies, projects and programmes.

We attach priority to the introduction of clean and low-waste technology, being aware of the need to support countries which do not yet have their own means for appropriate measures.

We underline that environmental policies should be supported by appropriate legislative measures and administrative structures to ensure their effective implementation.

We stress the need for new measures providing for the systematic evaluation of compliance with the existing commitments and, moreover, for the development of more ambitious commitments with regard to notification and exchange of information about the state of the environment and potential environmental hazards. We also welcome the creation of the European Environment Agency (EEA).

We welcome the operational activities, problem-oriented studies and policy reviews in various existing international organizations engaged in the protection of the environment, such as the United Nations Environment Programme (UNEP), the United Nations Economic Commission for Europe (ECE) and the Organisation for Economic Co-operation and Development (OECD). We emphasize the need for strengthening their co-operation and for their efficient co-ordination.

Culture

We recognize the essential contribution of our common European culture and our shared values in overcoming the division of the continent. Therefore, we underline our attachment to creative freedom and to the protection and promotion of our cultural and spiritual heritage, in all its richness and diversity.

In view of the recent changes in Europe, we stress the increased importance of the Cracow Symposium and we look forward to its consideration of guidelines for intensified co-operation in the field of culture. We invite the Council of Europe to contribute to this Symposium.

In order to promote greater familiarity amongst our peoples, we favour the establishment of cultural centres in cities of other participating States as well as increased co-operation in the audio-visual field and wider exchange in music, theatre, literature and the arts.

We resolve to make special efforts in our national policies to promote better understanding, in particular among young people, through cultural exchanges, co-operation in all fields of education and, more specifically, through teaching and training in the languages of other participating States. We intend to consider first results of this action at the Helsinki Follow-up Meeting in 1992.

Migrant Workers

We recognize that the issues of migrant workers and their families legally residing in host countries have economic, cultural and social aspects as well as their human dimension. We reaffirm that the protection and promotion of their rights, as well as the implementation of relevant international obligations, is our common concern.

Mediterranean

We consider that the fundamental political changes that have occurred in Europe have a positive relevance to the Mediterranean region. Thus, we will continue efforts to strengthen security and co-operation in the Mediterranean as an important factor for stability in Europe. We welcome the Report of the Palma de Mallorca Meeting on the Mediterranean, the results of which we all support.

We are concerned with the continuing tensions in the region, and renew our determination to intensify efforts towards finding just, viable and lasting solutions, through peaceful means, to outstanding crucial problems, based on respect for the principles of the Final Act.

We wish to promote favourable conditions for a harmonious development and diversification of relations with the non-participating Mediterranean States. Enhanced co-operation with these States will be pursued with the aim of promoting economic and social development and thereby enhancing stability in the region. To this end, we will strive together with these countries towards a substantial narrowing of the prosperity gap between Europe and its Mediterranean neighbours.

Non-governmental Organizations

We recall the major role that non-governmental organizations, religious and other groups and individuals have played in the achievement of the objectives of the CSCE and will further facilitate their activities for the implementation of the CSCE commitments by the participating States. These organizations, groups and individuals must be involved in an appropriate way in the activities and new structures of the CSCE in order to fulfil their important tasks.

New structures and institutions of the CSCE Process

Our common efforts to consolidate respect for human rights, democracy and the rule of law, to strengthen peace and to promote unity in Europe require a new quality of political dialogue and co-operation and thus development of the structures of the CSCE.

The intensification of our consultations at all levels is of prime importance in shaping our future relations. To this end, we decide on the following.

We, the Heads of State or Government, shall meet next time in Helsinki on the occasion of the CSCE Follow-up Meeting 1992. Thereafter, we will meet on the occasion of subsequent follow-up meetings.

Our Ministers for Foreign Affairs will meet, as a Council, regularly and at least once a year. These meetings will provide the central forum for political consultations within the CSCE process. The Council will consider issues relevant to the Conference on Security and Co-operation in Europe and take appropriate decisions.

The first meeting of the Council will take place in Berlin.

A Committee of Senior Officials will prepare the meetings of the Council and carry out its decisions. The Committee will review current issues and may take appropriate decisions, including in the form of recommendations to the Council.

Additional meetings of the representatives of the participating States may be agreed upon to discuss questions of urgent concern.

The Council will examine the development of provisions for convening meetings of the Committee of Senior Officials in emergency situations.

Meetings of other Ministers may also be agreed by the participating States.

In order to provide administrative support for these consultations we establish a Secretariat in Prague.

Follow-up meetings of the participating States will be held, as a rule, every two years to allow the participating States to take stock of developments, review the implementation of their commitments and consider further steps in the CSCE process.

We decide to create a Conflict Prevention Centre in Vienna to assist the Council in reducing the risk of conflict.

We decide to establish an Office for Free Elections in Warsaw to facilitate contacts and the exchange of information on elections within participating States.

Recognizing the important role parliamentarians can play in the CSCE process, we call for greater parliamentary involvement in the CSCE, in particular through the creation of a CSCE parliamentary assembly, involving members of parliaments from all participating States. To this end, we urge that contacts be pursued at parliamentary level to discuss the field of activities, working methods and rules of procedure of such a CSCE parliamentary structure, drawing on existing experience and work already undertaken in this field.

We ask our Ministers for Foreign Affairs to review this matter on the occasion of their first meeting as a Council.

*

Procedural and organizational modalities relating to certain provisions contained in the Charter of Paris for a New Europe are set out in the Supplementary Document which is adopted together with the Charter of Paris.

We entrust to the Council the further steps which may be required to ensure the implementation of decisions contained in the present document, as well as in the Supplementary Document, and to consider further efforts for the strengthening of security and co-operation in Europe. The Council may adopt any amendment to the supplementary document which it may deem appropriate.

*

The original of the Charter of Paris for a New Europe, drawn up in English, French, German, Italian, Russian and Spanish, will be transmitted to the Government of the French Republic, which will retain it in its archives. Each of the participating States will receive from the Government of the French Republic a true copy of the Charter of Paris.

The text of the Charter of Paris will be published in each participating State, which will disseminate it and make it known as widely as possible.

The Government of the French Republic is requested to transmit to the Secretary-General of the United Nations the text of the Charter of Paris for a New Europe which is not eligible for registration under Article 102 of the Charter of the United Nations, with a view to its circulation to all the members of the Organization as an official document of the United Nations.

ANNEXES

CHRONOLOGY

1972	31 May	The Member States of the North Atlantic Council agreed to the launching of multilateral talks concerning the preparation of a Conference on Security and Cooperation in Europe (CSCE).
	22 November	Opening of preparatory multilateral consultations at the CSCE in Helsinki.
1973	3 July	Opening of the first CSCE in Helsinki.
1975	1st August	Final act of the CSCE, called the Helsinki Final Act.
1989	6 March	Start of negotiations on conventional forces in Europe (CFE) in Vienna.
	9 March - 18 November 1990	Conference on Confidence- and Security-Building Measures and Disarmament in Europe and Vienna.
	20-21 May	Meeting of George H. W. Bush and François Mitterrand in Kennebunkport (Maine, United States).
	30 May - 23 June	Conference on the Human Dimension of the CSCE in Paris.
	14 June	Official visit by François Mitterrand to Poland.
	26-27 June	European Council Meeting in Madrid. In its conclusions, the European Council states that it "is convinced that the CSCE process provides the appropriate framework for achieving greater progress in all these fields [arms control and disarmament, respect for human rights and the free circulation of ideas, information and persons], enabling Europe to look forward to a day when its present divisions become a matter of history."
	July	July session of the Parliamentary Assembly of the Council of Europe in Strasbourg. First participation as "special guest" of delegations from Hungary, Poland, Yugoslavia and the Supreme Soviet of the USSR. Speech by Mikhail Gorbachev, General Secretary of the Communist Party of the Soviet Union before the Parliamentary Assembly and mention of the concept "Common European Home"
	25 September	Council of Europe Recommendation 1112 on East-West cooperation at the close of the twentieth century.
	16 October - 3 November	CSCE Meeting on the Protection of the Environment in Sofia.

ANNEXES

	9 November	Fall of the Berlin Wall.
	28 November	Helmut Kohl's Ten-Point Plan for German Unity.
	30 November	Declaration of Mikhail Gorbachev in Rome where he launched the idea of a summit of the 35 CSCE Participating States.
	6 December	Visit by François Mitterrand to Kiev. He announced his support for Mikhail Gorbachev's idea of holding a summit.
	8-9 December	European Council meeting in Strasbourg. Dual agreement on the principle of German reunification and the integration of the GDR in the EEC as well as the realization of the Economic and Monetary Union.
	16-29 December	Velvet Revolution in Czechoslovakia.
	22 December	Official visit by François Mitterrand to the GDR.
	22 December	Opening ceremony of Brandenburg Gate.
	31 December	François Mitterrand announced his European Confederation project.
1990	4 January	François Mitterrand received Helmut Kohl in Latché (Landes).
	6 February	Helmut Kohl proposed an Economic and Monetary Union with the GDR.
	10 February	Mikhail Gorbachev announced the USSR's agreement so that the FRG and the GDR could freely decide the reunification terms and conditions.
	February	Creation of a CSCE summit working group.
	12-13 February	Open Skies Conference in Ottawa.
	5 March	Mikhail Gorbachev was elected President of the USSR.
	9 March	Visit to Paris by Wojciech Jaruzelski, President of the Republic of Poland, and Tadeusz Mazowiecki, Prime Minister of the Republic of Poland. Meetings with François Mitterrand on the Oder-Neisse line and presence of Poland at the 2+4 Conference.
	19-20 March	Visit by Vaclav Havel to Paris.
	19 March - 11 April	CSCE Conference on Economic Co-operation in Europe in Bonn.
	30 March	Visit by Roland Dumas to Moscow.
	25-26 April	55th Franco-German Summit in Paris. Main issues addressed: achievements of the Franco-German Summit, the EEC, European security, German unification and Lithuania.
	28 April	Extraordinary European Council meeting in Dublin. Mainly dedicated to relations between the EEC and Eastern European countries.

ANNEXES

5 May	Opening of the 2+4 Conference in Bonn to settle international aspects of reunification.
8 May	Council of Europe Recommendation 1124 on the Relations with the countries of Central and Eastern Europe (General Policy of the Council of Europe).
25 May	Visit by François Mitterrand to Moscow.
29 May	Signing of the constitutive act of the European Bank for Reconstruction and Development (ERBD) in Paris.
5-29 June	Conference on the Human Dimension of the CSCE in Copenhagen.
5 June	Special Meeting of Foreign Ministers of CSCE Participating States. Decision taken on the establishment of a preparatory committee at the Summit to be held in Vienna starting 10 July.
21 June	The Bundestag and the Volkskammer proclaimed the definitive nature of the border with Poland.
25-26 June	European Council meeting in Dublin. Mainly focused on the situation in Eastern Europe and the possibility of economic assistance for the USSR, terms and conditions of German unification and Political Union of Europe.
1st July	Entry into force of the Economic, Monetary and Social Union between the GDR and the FRG.
5 July	French-German consultation on the CSCE in Bonn.
6 July	Meeting at the North Atlantic Council Summit in London on Western expectations for the future of the CSCE.
10-27 July	Preparatory Committee of the Summit meeting held in Vienna (first session).
13 July	European Parliament Resolution on the political evolution in Central and Eastern European countries, including the Soviet Union, and the role of the European Community.
17 July	Third 2+4 Conference in Paris.
23 August	Entry into force of the Act on the accession of the GDR to the area of validity of the Basic Law of the FRG by the GDR Parliament.
26-27 August	Visit by Roland Dumas to Moscow.
31 August	Signature of the Unification Treaty between the FRG and the GDR.
4 September - 18 November	Preparatory Committee of the Summit meeting held in Vienna (second session).
12 September	Treaty on the Final Settlement with Respect to Germany known as the Moscow Treaty (or 4+ or 2+4 Treaty). Agreement between representatives of the two Germanys, France, the United States, the United Kingdom and the USSR, paving the way for German reunification.

ANNEXES

	17-18 September	56th Franco-German Summit in Munich. François Mitterrand announced to Helmut Kohl that French troops would leave the country.
	18 September	Extraordinary Ministerial Session of the Western European Union (WEU).
	24 September - 18 October	CSCE Meeting on the Mediterranean in Palma de Mallorca.
	1st-2 October	Special Meeting of Foreign Ministers of CSCE Participating States in New York.
	3 October	German reunification.
	29 October	French-Soviet Treaty of Understanding and Cooperation signed in Paris.
	9 November	German-Soviet Treaty on Good Neighbourly Relations, Partnership and Cooperation signed in Bonn.
	14 November	Signature of the Treaty on the German-Polish Border in Warsaw.
	19 November	Signature of the Treaty on Conventional Armed Forces in Europe or CFE, in Paris, between 22 representatives of NATO and the Warsaw Pact States.
	19-21 November	Paris Summit, meeting of Heads of State and Government of CSCE Participating States.
	21 November	Signature of the Charter of Paris for a New Europe.
1991	15 January - 8 February	Meeting of Experts on the Peaceful Settlement of Disputes at La Valette.
	25 January	Dissolution of the military structures of the Warsaw Pact.
	13-14 June	European Prague Confederation Conference.
	9 April	French-Polish Treaty of Friendship and Solidarity signed in Paris.
	28 May - 7 June	Seminar on cultural heritage in Krakow.
	17 June	Signature of a Treaty on Good Neighbourship and Friendly Cooperation between Poland and Germany.
	19-20 June	First meeting of the CSCE Council in Berlin.
	19-21 August	Putsch in Moscow.
	10 September	Additional meeting of the CSCE Council (on the margins of the opening of the Conference on the Human Dimension of the CSCE) in Moscow. (Admission of the Baltic States: Estonia, Latvia and Lithuania).
	25 December	Resignation of Mikhail Gorbachev and dissolution of the USSR.
1992	30-31 January	Second meeting of the CSCE Council in Prague.
	10-20 March	Preparatory meeting of the fourth follow-up meeting, Helsinki. (Admission of Croatia, Georgia and Slovenia).

	24 March-8 July	CSCE fourth follow-up meeting in Helsinki.
	9-10 July	CSCE Summit in Helsinki.
	14-15 December	Third meeting of the CSCE Council of Ministers in Stockholm.
1993	5-6 December	CSCE Summit in Budapest.
1994	1st January	The CSCE became the OSCE: Organization for Security and Co-operation in Europe.

BIBLIOGRAPHY

ANDRÉANI Jacques, *Le piège : Helsinki et la chute du communisme*, Paris, Odile Jacob, 2005.

ASMUS Ronald D., *Opening NATO's Door. How the Alliance Remade Itself for a New Era*, Columbia University Press, 2002.

BADALASSI Nicolas, *En finir avec la Guerre froide : La France, l'Europe et le processus d'Helsinki, 1965-1975*, Rennes, Presses universitaires de Rennes, 2014.

BADALASSI Nicolas, SNYDER Sarah B. (dir.), *The CSCE and the End of the Cold War: Diplomacy, Societies and Human Rights*, 1972-1990, New York, Berghahn Books, 2018.

BOZO Frédéric, *Mitterrand, la fin de la Guerre froide et l'unification allemande, De Yalta à Maastricht*, Paris, Odile Jacob, 2005.

BOZO Frédéric, REY Marie-Pierre, LUDLOW N. Piers, NUTI Leopoldo (dir.), *Europe and the End of the Cold War: A Reappraisal*, Londres, Routledge, 2008.

BOZO Frédéric, REY Marie-Pierre, LUDLOW N. Piers, ROTHER Bernd (dir.), *Overcoming the Iron Curtain: Vision of the End of the Cold War, 1945-1990*, Berghahn Books, 2012.

BOZO Frédéric, WENKEL Christian (dir.), *France and the German Question, 1945-1990*, New York, Berghahn Books, 2019.

DECAUX Emmanuel, *La Conférence sur la sécurité et la coopération en Europe (CSCE)*, Paris, Presses universitaires de France, coll. « Que sais-je ? », 1992.

DECAUX Emmanuel, SUR Serge, *L'OSCE, trente ans après l'acte final de Helsinki. Sécurité coopérative et dimension humaine*, Paris, Pedone, 2008.

DUMAS Roland, *Politiquement incorrect. Secrets d'État et autres confidences. Carnets 1984-2014*, Paris, Le Cherche-Midi, 2015.

FOUCHER Michel, *Fronts et frontières*, Paris, Fayard, 1988.

GENSCHER Hans-Dietrich, *Erinnerungen*, Berlin, Siedler Verlag, 1995.

GHEBALI Victor-Yves, *La diplomatie de la détente. La CSCE, d'Helsinki à Vienne (1973-1989)*, Bruxelles, Bruylant, 1989.

GHEBALI Victor-Yves, *L'OSCE dans l'Europe post-communiste 1990-1996 : Vers une identité paneuropéenne de sécurité*, Bruxelles, Bruylant, 1996.

GHEBALI Victor-Yves, LAMBERT Alexandre, *The OSCE Code of Conduct on Politico-Military Aspects of Security: Anatomy and Implementation*, Leiden, Martinus Nijhoff Publishers, 2005.

GHEBALI Victor-Yves, LAMBERT Alexandre, *Democratic Governance of the Security Sector beyond the OSCE Area: Regional Approaches in Africa and the Americas*, DCAF (LIT), Geneva/Zurich/Vienna, 2007.

GROSSER Pierre, *1989, l'année où le monde a basculé*, Paris, Perrin, 2009.

GROSSER Pierre, *Les temps de la Guerre froide. Réflexions sur l'histoire de la Guerre froide et les causes de sa fin*, Bruxelles, Complexe, 1995.

KWASCHIK Anne, PFEIL Ulrich (dir.), *Die DDR in den deutsch-französischen Beziehungen*, Bruxelles, Peter Lang, 2013.

MARESCA John J., PASHAYEV Hafiz, UMLAND Andreas, *Helsinki revisited: A Key U.S. Negotiator's Memoirs on the Development of the CSCE into the OSCE (Soviet and Post-Soviet Politics and Society)*, Ibidem Press, 2016.

SCHABERT Tilo, *Mitterrand et la réunification allemande, Une histoire secrète (1981-1995)*, Paris, Grasset, 2005 [version française remaniée et augmentée de l'ouvrage de langue allemande : *Wie Weltgeschichte gemacht wird*].

VÉDRINE Hubert, *Les Mondes de François Mitterrand. À l'Élysée de 1981 à 1995*, Paris, Fayard, 1996.

PHOTOGRAPHY CREDITS

All the documents presented are property of the Ministry for Europe and Foreign Affairs and are kept in the Archives Centre of the Ministry for Europe and Foreign Affairs, La Courneuve, image collection.

All the photographs were taken by Frédéric de la Mure unless otherwise specified.

p. 9 A051302, p. 43 A051363, p. 46 P010409, p. 51 A051368, p. 54 © Olivier Ezratty, p. 57 A051304, p. 59 A051330, p. 67 A051309, p. 69 A040970 © Loiseleur des Lonchamps, p. 79 A051307, p. 84 P011888, p. 89 A051366, p. 91 personal collection Mr Perrin de Brichambaut, p. 95 P011928, p. 99 A051310, p. 101 personal collection Mr Champenois, p. 107 A051308, p. 109 P011919.

Photographs

A051316, A051317, A051323, A051306, A051305, A051303, A051290, A051300, A051301, A051328, A051325, A051365, A051369, contact sheet A051344r, A051367, contact sheet A051344R, A051364, contact sheet A051345r, Audiovisual Collection, AV664

Charter of Paris © Tristan Happel/MEAE

p. 145 Treaties, TRA19900027.001.127, TRA19900027.001.128, TRA19900027.001.129, TRA19900027.001.130, TRA19900027.001.131, TRA19900027.001.132, TRA19900027.001.133, TRA19900027.001.134, TRA19900027.001.135, TRA19900027.001.136, TRA19900027.001.137, TRA19900027.001.138, TRA19900027.001.138, TRA19900027.001.139, TRA19900027.001.139, TRA19900027.001.140, TRA19900027.001.141, TRA19900027.001.142, TRA19900027.001.143, TRA19900027.001.12144.

TABLE OF CONTENTS

PREFACE 3

THE CHARTER OF PARIS AND THE HISTORY OF THE END OF THE COLD
WAR. 5

MITTERRAND'S VISION AND THE END OF THE COLD WAR 17

THE "*MAGNA CARTA* OF FREEDOM" THE CHARTER OF PARIS IN THE
HISTORY OF THE CSCE 31

TESTIMONIALS 43
- The oral archives campaign about the Charter of Paris. 44
- Hubert VÉDRINE 46
- Jean MUSITELLI. 54
- Pierre MOREL 69
- Sophie-Caroline de MARGERIE 76
- Michel FOUCHER. 84
- Marc PERRIN DE BRICHAMBAUT. 91
- Lucien CHAMPENOIS. 101

ILLUSTRATIONS BOOK

UNPUBLISHED ARCHIVES OF THE PREPARATORY COMMITTEE NEGOTIA-
TIONS IN VIENNA. 109

CONCLUSION 141

TABLE OF CONTENTS

- ANNEXES 143
  - Paris Summit Programme 143
  - Charter of Paris 145
  - Chronology 153
  - Bibliography 159
  - Photography Credits 161

This book was jointly published
by the Diplomatic Archives Directorate,
Ministry for Europe and Foreign Affairs,
3 rue Suzanne Masson, 93120 La Courneuve
The CTHS, Campus Condorcet, 14 cours des Humanités,
93320 Aubervilliers Cedex
The Comité des Travaux Historiques et Scientifiques
is an institute affiliated with the École National des Chartes

COMPOGRAVURE
IMPRESSION, BROCHAGE

CHIRAT
Imprimeur - Relieur

42540 ST-JUST-LA-PENDUE
OCTOBER 2020
REGISTRATION OF COPYRIGHT 2020
No. 202010.0086

PRINTED IN FRANCE